To my very special
nephew whom I love
very much. Congratul—
on your graduation.
Aunt Linda
6-23-96

I hope the southern side of
you enjoy this book!

The
South Carolina
Story

The South Carolina Story

by Anne Riggs Osborne

Sandlapper Publishing, Inc.

Orangeburg, South Carolina

Sandlapper Publishing, Inc.
P.O. Drawer 730
Orangeburg, South Carolina 29116-0730

Library of Congress Cataloging-in-Publication Data

Osborne, Anne (Anne Riggs)
The South Carolina story.

Bibliography: p.
Includes index.
1. South Carolina—History.   I. Title.
F269.08   1988   975.7   87-37628
ISBN 0-87844-083-6
ISBN 0-87844-104-2 (pbk).

Contents

Foreword

The South Carolina Story is, I hope, an easy-reading history. It is not beamed at any particular age group, but is written as I would write a newspaper or magazine article, in simple language and uncomplicated prose.

I have not written for economists or sociologists or serious historians, but for casual readers. A lover of historical fiction, an eighth-grade social studies student or a tourist, new to Carolina, may get some background for his or her particular interest of the moment. If any want to read from cover to cover, I hope the narrative moves fast enough to hold the reader's interest.

As a novelist, I have always been more interested in the people who have made history, and I have concentrated on the human side in this book. In such a short account, it has been impossible to include everybody who influenced South Carolina's formation, so I have highlighted a few characters, some bad and some good, who struck my fancy. If they are out of proportion to their importance, particularly the pirates, it is because I know and love them best.

I have tried to be unbiased. I have read all sides of controversial subjects and have written as fairly as anyone can who was raised on Joel Chandler Harris and Thomas Nelson Page, and who has lived most of her adult life in Georgia and the Carolinas. I have tried to give a full picture of slavery so that black Carolinians may know something of their ancestors, who were among the earliest colonists, and may feel pride in their contribution to Carolina's growth.

Not a native Carolinian and a novelist rather than historian, I have tried to be sure of my facts. I want to thank the several South Carolinians who read and made suggestions about my manuscript, especially Ms. Rose Till, a retired history teacher from Orangeburg, and the Reverend Allen B. Clarkson, who is descended from everyone of importance in South Carolina, beginning with Henry Woodward, and put me straight on several dreadful mistakes.

The reading lists at the end of the book should give the reader clues to further explorations on any period or person that catches his fancy. At least some of these books can be found in most public libraries. May they help to encourage a love of history.

Anne Osborne

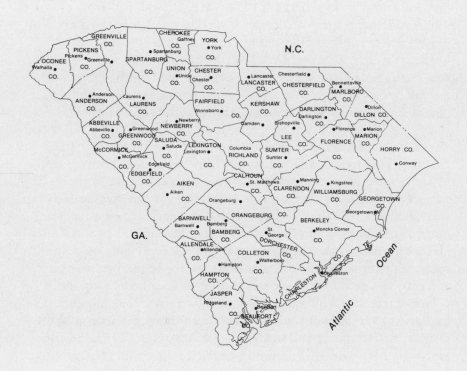

Before the Dawn
of History

Long before the beginning of recorded history, the red hills of South Carolina were born. A part of the Ocoees, a range of mountains that stretched from present-day Virginia to the Gulf of Mexico, they were higher than the Alps are today. Over the next 300 million years, conditions changed; floods and winds and ice and more upheavals of the earth wore the mountains down until they became what are now the hills of the Carolina Piedmont, some of the oldest hills on earth.

Two hundred million years ago, west of the old Ocoees, another upheaval took place, throwing up the Appalachian range, of which the Blue Ridge Mountains are a part. During this period, the sea came up the very edge of the Piedmont hills. In the next hundred million years, the sea moved down to what is known as the continental shelf, 150 miles beyond today's Atlantic coastline. Receding from among the hills of the Ocoees, the waters formed rivers which crossed the plains into the ocean. In the hills and plains, by this time, life had come to the earth, and reptiles and insects lived along the riverbanks in forests of fern-like trees. This was the age of the dinosaurs, and although these huge creatures have been extinct for thousands of years, the descendants of that prehistoric age, turtles and alligators, still live in the rivers and swamps of today.

During the millions of years between Earth's formation and man's emergence, there were long periods of extreme heat alternating with extreme cold when great sheets of ice would form on parts of the

Earth's surface and then melt, to be replaced many years later by other sheets of ice. When the ice melted, the oceans would rise and cover great stretches of land. One such flood is believed to have caused the ocean to rise and cover all the fern forests of Carolina up to the foot of the old Ocoees, which were worn down almost to the rolling Piedmont hills of today. This new shoreline was parallel to what is now South Carolina's coastline and lay about half-way between the state's present coastline and mountains. It is known today as the Fall Line.

During this period the sea covered half of what is now South Carolina, and on its shore were sand dunes and sandy beaches. Today, 100 miles from the sea, shells of huge oysters and prehistoric sharks' teeth are found in Up-Country springs. The sea finally fell to somewhere near its present shore, leaving a great line of sand hills from Augusta, Georgia through Columbia and northward across the state. The rivers of South Carolina also show the influence of prehistory. Rushing down from the Blue Ridge, they follow the winding courses that once cut through the Ocoees—now the Piedmont. As they come to the Fall Line, they straighten out and move leisurely on to the sea.

It was into this country of rolling red hills, sandy pine barrens and murky swamps that prehistoric man first came.

Very little is known of the first Carolina inhabitants, the Paleo-Indians. It is believed that man first came to the Western Hemisphere across the Bering Straits and then proceeded across the continent; the first Carolinians came from the west over 12,000 years ago. Very few traces have been found of their lifestyle—only crude, leaf-shaped knives or spearpoints chipped from stone. They probably lived on nuts, fruit and game, and moved from place to place where food was found. Perhaps they trapped and killed the elephant-like mammoths of the time. What few artifacts they left behind are found mainly on hilltop sites. What became of these people, or whether they were related to later inhabitants, no one knows.

Around 8000 B.C. another group of people came to live in Carolina, staying closer to the riverbanks than the Paleo-Indians. Some of these Archaic People lived on an island in the Savannah River near present-day North Augusta, South Carolina for many generations. A pit in the center of the island had been used as a garbage dump, or "midden," for centuries. Because the island was isolated and no one had dug there before, the Peabody Institute of Harvard was able, in the 1920s, to make careful excavations and take out layer after layer of broken pottery, bones, shells and discarded household objects. From the layers at the very bottom of the pit, it was found that the earliest of these people came to the river to catch fish and kill the animals who drank there. They lived on fish, shellfish, small animals, wild roots and wild grains, using notched bone spear-throwers, grooved axes and crude mortars for milling grain. They made grit-tempered pottery which they decorated by digging a stick into the clay before it dried.

These "Savannah River People" had round skulls, unlike the long-headed people of the Woodland Era who followed them. They were the first people known by archeology to have kept dogs as pets. Then suddenly, before the dawn of history as we know it, they disappeared without a trace.

The long-headed Woodland People who came to Carolina about 1000 B.C. vanished before white men came but left behind them mounds and earthworks which were still being used in the sixteenth century, although the Indians of that time knew nothing about the original builders. These stone and earth mounds, many like pyramids with flattened tops, can still be found along the Santee River and its tributaries and up into the hills of north Georgia. Archeologists still puzzle over them. Some were used as burial grounds, some had temples on top, and some had both graves and temples. Some which had neither may have been fortifications to keep out enemies.

The Woodland mound builders apparently believed that man's spirit went on after death. A skeleton found in one of the burial mounds, that of a warrior who lived about 700 years ago, was buried with colored war paint, pieces of mica and round "game stones," which were used in a primitive type of bowling. Other skeletons have been found which were half burned and sealed in burial urns; these large clay pots always had a hole broken in them (known as "killing" the jars) so that the soul could escape.

The Woodland People did most of their cooking over open fires. They made stews by placing vegetables and meat in a large basket lined with clay or in a clay bowl, adding water, and then putting in stones that had been heated in a fire. These stones were doughnut-shaped and could be pulled out of the fire by putting a curved stick through the hole. It is believed that the Woodland culture reached its peak about 700 A.D. Like the Archaic Savannah River People, the long-heads of the Santee area disappeared, leaving only their mounds behind.

A burial urn (top) and (from left to right) an ax head, spear point, two arrow heads, set of trade beads, and two trade pipes. Photograph courtesy of South Carolina State Museum.

The Carolina
Indians

In the sixteenth century, when the Spanish first came to North America, they found the Indians here to be far different from the ones they had met in the Caribbean and farther south. The tribes of North America were more independent and liberty-loving, without the strong government systems of the Aztecs and Incas.

In the northwestern corner of present-day South Carolina was the Cherokee Nation, a group who had left the Great Lakes region and their kinsmen, the Iroquois, to settle in the warmer Blue Ridge Mountains and Piedmont hills. To the west, along the Savannah River and across what is now Georgia, were the Muskogean tribes, called Creeks by the English because they made their homes along creeks and rivers. Some of these tribes, the Yemassees and Cusabos, lived on the Carolina side of the Savannah as it approached the sea. The Seminoles, another Muskogean people, lived on the peninsula that is now Florida. The Creeks had been fighting the Cherokees over hunting lands for years, but they generally used Long Canes Creek as a dividing line.

In the east, along the present North Carolina border, the Iroquoian Tuscaroras and the coastal Algonquian tribes guarded their rights to hunt and fish the land. In the center of these hostile tribes were the river people of Sioux ancestry: the Sewees, Winyas, Congarees, Catawbas and Washaws who left their names to waterways where they lived. Legend tells of a battle between these people and the

Cherokees in the west, and of a truce that made the Broad River the boundary between the nations.

With four powerful nations constantly warring in this region, it is not surprising that the Indian population never grew very large. When the first Europeans came to America, they brought smallpox and other diseases along; the Indians, who had never been exposed to these diseases, died in great numbers. By the time the English came to colonize in the seventeenth century, there were no more than 25,000 Indians in the two Carolinas combined (not enough to fill a football stadium for a big game nowadays).

Over the centuries these Native Americans had learned to plant crops and weave baskets and cloth, and to cure pelts and sew them together to make clothing. About 300 years before the Europeans arrived, they had learned to string a bow, first to use as a musical instrument like a one-string guitar, and then to shoot sharp-pointed flint-tipped arrows.

As they learned to grow food, these tribes began to build permanent shelters where they could stay to cultivate and pick the crops. These Eastern Indians didn't use the cone-shaped folding teepees of the nomadic Plains Indians. Their houses were sturdily built and clustered in villages near a stream, usually on a bluff above flood level. The small huts were often shaped like half a ball with rounded tops for the rain to run off. The Indians made a frame of small, flexible trees which were implanted in the ground in a circle, bent and tied overhead to make an arched ceiling. Then thin branches were wrapped around the arch, and bark and skins were tied on to make walls.

Buildings varied from tribe to tribe, but most villages had the same general plan. The larger Indian towns were surrounded by palisades built of logs driven into the ground and fastened together with vines. In the center of the village was usually an open space for games and dancing. A large oblong building at one end of the open space was used for ceremonial occasions, often serving as a home for the chief and his family. Sometimes this building was on a mound. In many villages and towns each family or clan had a summer house, a winter house, and storage shelters built close together in a unit. The summer house was built of branches with open spaces between to let in air; the winter house was much like an igloo: round, made of tightly woven branches and covered with a thick layer of mud. There were no windows and only a small hole in the roof to let smoke escape, the entrance was through a low, curved corridor that cut off drafts. In Indian houses in the South, sleeping couches were built around the walls, two feet above the floor, away from snakes and too high for fleas to hop.

There were no horses or other beasts of burden in North America until the Spaniards came with their horses and mules. Men and women carried packs on their backs. Women also carried their babies on their backs, bound to wooden cradle boards; they hung the cradles on branches as they worked in the fields.

Religion varied in forms of celebration, but all believed in a Force that ruled Nature. Animals, rocks, plants and winds, as part of Nature, were believed to have spirits like men. The Indians tried to stay on the good side of Nature so they would not incur the wrath of the elements.

Most tribes were governed by chiefs or "Micos" who passed the office down through the female side of the family. A chief could be deposed if he made too many bad decisions.

Next to the Chief ranked several Second Men and then the Warriors. The Second Men oversaw such public works as the building of houses for newlyweds and portioning out work in the fields. They were also in charge of brewing Black Drink, a concoction of holly leaves and bark that was strong in caffeine and was drunk by all the grown men when they met to decide matters of state. (Sort of a coffee break at a primitive board meeting.) The Warriors were ranked according to their warlike feats, and a Great Warrior was designated as Chief in time of war. Great Warriors also arranged for ball games with other tribes in times of peace.

Most decisions of importance were decided in a council of adult males, where any member of the tribe could speak and matters were discussed until a consensus was reached. Rather than coercing those who disagreed, the council continued the discussion until everyone either agreed or withdrew.

The European
Explorers

The first Europeans known to have come to South Carolina were Spanish. At the end of the fifteenth century, Columbus had shown the people of the Old World that there were new and rich lands over the western horizon, ripe for the taking. Young men with a love of adventure signed aboard the tiny ships fitted out by Spanish grandees and sailed west to seek their fortunes. Sailing among the islands of the Caribbean and along the Spanish mainland of Central America and Mexico, the Spanish soon set up a trading empire, sending gold and raw materials back to Spain.

In 1520 an adventurer named Lucas Vasquez de Ayllon, who had settled on the island of Hispaniola (now Santo Domingo) and become a wealthy planter, decided to send an expedition to the mainland north of the peninsula now known as Florida. This northern mainland had been discovered accidentally by Juan Ponce de Leon, the governor of Puerto Rico, in 1513, when his ship was driven ashore there on Easter Sunday (*Pascha Floridium* in Latin). For many years the North American coast from Key West to Virginia was called *La Florida* by the Spaniards.

Ayllon himself remained in Hispaniola, but his captain, Francisco Gordillo, explored the coast of La Florida and beyond, as far north as present-day New York. Gordillo had been instructed not to make captives of any of the inhabitants and was sailing back to Hispaniola when he was hailed by a ship under the command of his cousin, a man named Quexos, who was setting out from Hispaniola to hunt for slaves. The Spaniards had worked the Carib Indians of the island so hard that they were dying by the thousands, and replacements were needed.

Quexos persuaded Gordillo to go back to the mainland with him, and on June 24, 1521 the two ships put into the mouth of a river at latitude 33° 30′ which they named San Juan Batisto, since it was Saint John the Baptist's Day. The Indians living here called the area Chicora. Today it is called Georgetown.

The Chicorans had never seen sailing ships before and thought they were great winged birds. They fled in terror from the men in shining armor. A single man and woman, who were curious and lagged behind, were taken aboard ship, dressed in fine European clothes and invited to feast on rich food. Then the Spaniards set them ashore to return to their friends, while Gordillo and Quexos took formal possession of the territory in the name of the Catholic King of Spain, carving crosses on the live oaks on the riverbank.

When the first two Indians returned to the river with 150 more, all hoping for the treatment the first two had received, the whole crowd was taken prisoner and the ships set out to sea. A few days later Quexos' ship sank in a storm, killing all aboard. The Indians on the other ship were so afraid that most of them starved themselves to death. When Gordillo's ship reached Hispaniola, Ayllon was furious with his captain for taking slaves but excited over the discovery of the San Juan Batisto River. Taking with him one of the few surviving Indians, whom he named Francisco of Chicora, Ayllon set off for Spain to ask the King's permission to explore the northern mainland.

Francisco of Chicora seems to have been a joker with a lively imagination. Spanish historians of the day repeat his tales of gigantic kings of Chicora who had been fed strange herbs as babies, so their bones were softened and could be stretched like dough. He told another story of a tribe of Indians with long, rigid tails who had to dig holes in the ground in order to sit comfortably. The Spaniards believed these and other tales of riches and marvels in North America. Emperor Charles V (Carlos I of Spain) sent Ayllon back to Chicora with an expedition of 500 white adventurers, a few black slaves, some Dominican friars and eighty-nine horses, the first to come to Carolina.

Ayllon's expedition formed in Hispaniola in July 1526 and arrived in the Cape Fear region of the coast in August, spending several

weeks looking for a passage to the Orient. Ayllon thought that
America was a narrow isthmus and that a river might lead through
to the Pacific Ocean. Finally, giving up that notion, he decided to
establish a town farther south, at the mouth of what the Spaniards
called the River Jordan (probably on Waccamaw Neck). The town,
known as San Miguel Gualdape, was not a success. The Spaniards
did not want to fish and plant food for themselves and the Indians,
though friendly at first, refused to be slaves and started killing the
white men. Fevers (probably malaria and yellow fever) were followed
by a bitter winter of starvation. Ayllon died during the winter, and
the colonists refused to follow his successor. Finally, the 150 Spaniards who survived of the original 500 gave up and sailed back to
Hispaniola.

It was fourteen years before Spain again sent adventurers to
Carolina, and this time they were only passing through in their
search for gold. Landing in Florida, Hernando De Soto and 500
soldiers, most of them on horseback, traveled up the coast to the
mouth of the Savannah River, then along its bank to what is now
Augusta, Georgia. Along the way De Soto asked Indians about gold
and was told that a beautiful Indian queen ruled a kingdom on both
sides of the river and had council houses encrusted with gold and
pearls. This Lady of Cofitachequi, whose town is thought to have
been at Silver Bluff, on the Carolina side of the river, welcomed the
Spaniards with open arms, presenting De Soto with a great string
of pearls from around her own neck. De Soto and his men were
transported across the river in canoes and given everything they
requested—except gold. In the council house of an abandoned village
they were allowed to take chests full of pearls but found that the
"gold" on the walls was mica and copper. Perhaps it was gold, said
Cofitachequi, that people were mining in the mountains to the
northwest; she suggested that De Soto should leave her village and
go there.

After accepting Cofitachequi's generous gifts and provisions for
500 soldiers, De Soto kidnapped the queen and moved his army off
toward the Piedmont hills.

The Gentleman of Elvas, one of the adventurers who wrote about
the expedition when he returned to Spain, says that "a dark man
from Africa" who had come with De Soto helped the queen escape
and conducted her back to Cofitachequi village, where he lived as

her consort and co-ruler thereafter. De Soto wandered through the foothills of the Blue Ridge and on into Tennessee. Still searching, he finally reached the banks of the Mississippi River where he died, a victim of his own lust for gold.

Twenty years later, another Spaniard named Angel de Villafane set out to colonize the coast of La Florida, landing on St. Helen's Day in 1561 at what is now Hilton Head, and naming the land Santa Elena in honor of the day. Villafane became discouraged with the land, which he thought unfit for a colony and sailed on to the north and, finally, back to Spain.

But though Spain had lost interest in settling La Florida and turned its attention to the gold of Mexico and Peru, France, on the other hand, had become fired with a desire to colonize.

In France, Protestants known as Huguenots were being persecuted as heretics by the Roman Catholic Church, and were seeking to escape. In February 1562, a Huguenot named Jean Ribaut sailed from Dieppe in Picardy with 150 men, hoping to establish a sanctuary for French Protestants in the New World. Reaching the coast of present-day Florida, the Frenchmen sailed northward until they came to the bay that Villafane had named Santa Elena. They were so impressed with the beauty of the country that they named the whole area Port Royal. This was truly a haven of refuge.

Ribaut stayed for over a month to supervise the building of a fortified settlement—named "Charlesfort" for the boy king, Charles IX of France—on what is now Parris Island. He then sailed for France to bring back more colonists and provisions. When Ribaut reached his homeland, however, he found the country torn by religious war and Admiral Coligny, who had sponsored his trip, out of office. Ribaut then went to the Protestant Queen Elizabeth of England, supposing that she might like to use Port Royal as a base for operations against Spain. Instead, he was thrown into prison, suspected of planning to turn an English expedition over to France.

Meanwhile, the thirty men who had been left at Charlesfort with guns, provisions and tools for farming had, like the Spaniards, grown lazy. Instead of planting crops and building sturdy houses, they depended on the friendly Indians of the area for food and shelter. When Ribaut failed to return, they built a small ship with the help of the Indians—who were probably glad to get rid of them, since they had eaten most of the Indian's winter stores. Shirts and sheets were used to make sails, and moss was used for caulking. In January 1563 they set sail, with plenty of guns for defense but not enough food to keep them from starving. Finally, after eating shoe leather and jackets and even turning to cannibalism, a few survivors were picked up by an English ship. The first French colony in Carolina had failed as miserably as the Spanish ones.

In 1564 Rene de Laudonierre, one of Ribaut's colonists from the Charlesfort days, tried again to establish a Huguenot colony in America—this time near what is now Jacksonville, Florida, on the St. John's River. The settlement was named Fort Caroline. Ribaut, now out of the English prison, brought a fleet to aid in establishing the colony. The Spaniards had paid little attention to the northern mainland, but they certainly did not want the French to settle so close to their interests. Hurrying up from the Caribbean Islands, the fierce Pedro Menendez de Aviles led an expedition against the French settlement, destroying it completely and cruelly killing the Huguenot colonists. Ribaut's fleet arrived in time to exchange shots with Menendez but was blown away and shipwrecked by a hurricane. The Spaniards, finding Ribaut and his shipwrecked crew, killed them.

The next year, to make sure that the French were discouraged from colonizing, Menendez founded St. Augustine, the first permanent settlement in what is now the United States, near Laudonierre's old colony. The following year, in order to assure a Spanish presence, he founded a string of mission-forts up the coast at Santa Elena-Charlesfort-Parris Island, naming this first mission San Felipe for the patron saint of Phillip II of Spain. The Edisto Indians, who had aided Ribaut's men, now helped the Spaniards to erect mission buildings and fortifications. It was here that "tabby"—a building material made from crushed oyster shells—was first developed. The Indians were converted by the Catholic priests and worked in the mission gardens and vineyards.

It was from San Felipe, in 1566, that Juan Pardo was sent by Menendez as an expedition scout to the Up Country. With a party of 150 men, he explored Carolina from the coast to the Blue Ridge, leaving an account of his travels that describes inland Carolina for the first time. Welcomed by friendly Indians all along the way, he did his best to "seek alliance with the natives, spread the gospel to the heathen," and open a trail from Santa Elena to Mexico.

Pardo describes fertile land, full-flowing rivers and mines of crystal that he thought were diamonds. Unlike De Soto, he repaid the Indians' hospitality with gifts and friendship, and tried to tell them about his God and his king. When he retraced his footsteps to San Felipe, leaving his sergeant, Boyano, in command of a fort in the Catawba valley, he was welcomed all along the way by throngs of Indians bearing gifts of maize, venison and chestnuts.

By the time Pardo returned to the Up Country, however, Boyano had taken an expedition on toward Mexico. Like many other Spanish conquistadores, Boyano had slaughtered Indians and burned villages whenever they resisted his commands. Heartsick, Pardo followed a thousand-mile trail of murder and pillage, then started back toward San Felipe, stopping to build blockhouses along the way and leaving a few Spaniards in each fort.

The Spaniards at San Felipe, meanwhile, had so angered the Edisto Indians that they went on the warpath, killing many and driving the rest off to St. Augustine, including Juan Pardo. Sergeant Boyano returned later, only to be killed by an Indian. What became of the defenders of Pardo's Up-Country forts is a matter of conjecture. A stone found near Inman, South Carolina is marked 1567 and is known as the Pardo Stone.

The Pardo Stone with carved date "1567," and other markings. Photograph courtesy of South Carolina Department of Archives and History.

By 1586, not only France but also England was challenging the might of Spain. Sir Francis Drake, after his great voyage around the world in the service of Elizabeth I of England, attacked St. Augustine with a force of twenty-five ships and 2,000 men and burned the town. Spain was forced to close the forts along the coast and concentrate on rebuilding and strengthening St. Augustine. After the English fleet, under Drake, destroyed the Spanish Armada in 1588, Spain was never again strong enough to extend her empire into North America. Carolina was wide open for settlement by England and the Protestant French.

The Proprietary
Colony

After Drake destroyed the Spanish navy in the English Channel, Spain no longer ruled the sea lanes. Gold, silver and jewels were still being taken out of Central and South America to fill the Spanish treasury, but North America had yielded no such riches. The Spaniards chose to protect their treasure fleets, which passed close to the Florida peninsula on their voyage home, and pull back their soldiers from the Carolina coast.

Phillip II of Spain sent Menendez back to St. Augustine, to rebuild the city burned by Drake and build a strong fort and naval base there. The Spanish missions farther north were slowly abandoned over the next 100 years.

Although it was many years before England sent colonists to Carolina, English ships ranged the Carolina coast at will, using the sea islands and inlets as bases for attack on Spanish fleets. When England was at war with Spain, they sailed as privateers, under commissions from the English Crown. Much of the time, however, when England was supposed to be at peace with Spain, these sea dogs were actually pirates. News of war and peace traveled slowly, and their method was to attack first and ask questions later.

Early in the seventeenth century, England began colonizing the islands of the Caribbean. As pirate hangouts, these islands were more secluded than the coast of Carolina, and although Spain claimed sovereignty over all the West Indies, English ships had been buccaneering among the islands for fifty years or so. Sir Francis

Drake himself had been called a pirate and Sir Henry Morgan, later to become governor of Jamaica, made his start as a buccaneer.

These early adventurers were not interested in colonization. Often they would drop members of their crews off on the islands to catch wild goats and pigs and smoke them to make *boucan* (the jerked meat from which the name buccaneer derived), or pull their ships into hidden bays to careen and clean their hulls. But as Spain's power became less and England's grew, English, French and Dutch colonists began to settle in the islands, agreeing among themselves which islands would belong to what country, and all allied against the Spanish. Between 1604 and 1640 the English settled on several islands, but Barbados was by far their most successful colony.

Located far south and outside the ring of Caribbean islands, Barbados was suited for agriculture, and it was the first stop for ships coming from Africa. The first colonists planted tobacco for export and vegetables to feed themselves, but in 1640 their simple life ended with the introduction of sugar cane, a money crop in any European market. Slave labor was needed for cultivation, and the shores of Africa were not far away. In no time, Barbados was *the* place to go to get rich in a hurry, and more and more colonists flocked to the 166-square-mile island, buying more and more black Africans to till their fields.

With Spanish attention on St. Augustine and points south and Barbados overflowing, Carolina was ripe for English colonization. Besides, England had a refugee problem. Hundreds of Huguenots had fled to Protestant England. They were treated hospitably, but they created an unemployment problem in the crowded English cities. To solve the problem, Robert Heath, King Charles' Attorney General, proposed a colony to which the Huguenots could be sent, with all revenues returned to England.

In 1629, Heath was granted all the territory between Florida and Virginia by Charles I of England, completely ignoring the Spanish claim. The land was to be called "Carolana" from *Carolus I Rex*, Charles' Latin title. Jamestown, Virginia had already been founded in 1607 when Charles' father, James I, was king; and Plymouth, Massachusetts had been settled by the Mayflower Pilgrims in 1620.

Brochures were printed in London, telling of the wonders of Carolana; some of them made modern promotion schemes seem tame by comparison. In 1630 the *Mayflower* sailed for the New

World once more, this time loaded with Huguenots bound for Carolana. For some unknown reason, however, they were landed in Virginia and settled there instead.

Meanwhile, England was in political and religious turmoil. The forces of Parliament under the leadership of Puritan Oliver Cromwell were in revolt against the Anglican king, Charles I. Englishmen were too busy fighting a civil war at home to colonize America. Charles was defeated and beheaded in 1649, and for ten stormy years Cromwell's men ruled England. Their laws were so strict that the people of England rebelled after Cromwell's death in 1658; two years later the young Charles Stuart, son of Charles I, was restored to the throne.

Charles II brought in an era of luxury after ten years of war and strict moral and social regulation. Supporters who had helped him to the throne would be paid with land and titles, and there was a whole continent to be given away in the New World. A colony should be founded to carry on the glorious society of Stuart England.

Robert Heath's charter, which had never been used, was now cancelled. Eight noblemen, known as the Lords Proprietors, were given a charter to the colony to be called Carolina. They would be responsible for the building and governing of the colony and would divide any profits among themselves. All of them were rich and powerful noblemen, and all hoped to become richer through colonial trade. They were: Edward Hyde, Earl of Clarendon; George Monck, Duke of Albemarle; William, Lord Craven; John, First Baron Berkeley; Sir William Berkeley (his brother); Sir John Colleton; Sir George Carteret; and Anthony Ashley-Cooper, Earl of Shaftesbury.

Ashley-Cooper had more influence on early planning for the colony than any of the other proprietors. With liberal ideas far ahead of his time, he commissioned John Locke, a philosopher, to write a constitution for the colony, giving more religious and political freedom than was enjoyed by any other colony. On the other hand, Locke believed in aristocracy, and his rules for a social system seem unbelievable in America today.

Locke's constitution, in order to avoid democracy, set up a feudal system, making nobles of the landowners, with the highest rank called *landgraves*, the next rank *caciques*. Each nobleman was to receive 12,000 acres to be worked by commoners known as *leetmen*. These leetmen and all their descendants were to remain leetmen forever, with no chance to change their class. The noblemen, along with the Proprietors (most of whom remained in England), were to make up the Council and should have a veto over any laws made by the elected Assembly.

Although Locke's Fundamental Constitution was considered an experiment in liberalism at the time, the whole plan for settlement was actually a money-making proposition. The Proprietors were less interested in spreading English civilization or helping refugees than in making fortunes in agriculture and trade. Their grant from Charles II specified that the king should receive rent from them, as well as one-fourth of all gold and silver found in Carolina. Most of the Proprietors remained in England and never saw the New World. Five of them were on the Board of Trade, and six on the Council of Foreign Plantations.

Ashley-Cooper, Hyde and Colleton already had property in Barbados, and William Berkeley was an ex-governor of Virginia. Unwilling to spend a great deal of money on building the colony or transporting immigrants, the Proprietors tried propaganda to attract settlers. Promotional literature again flowed from English presses, this time describing Carolina as a paradise and claiming, "If any maid or single woman have a desire to go over, they will think themselves in the Golden Age,—for if they be but Civil, and under 50 years of Age, some honest Man will purchase them for wives." But without financial backing, colonists failed to flock aboard ship, even old maids.

In 1663, a group of Barbadian planters, anxious to start plantations on the mainland, commissioned Captain William Hilton to explore the Carolina coast. Hilton had been to the Cape Fear region the year before; now he sailed farther south to Port Royal, then went back to Barbados to publish a pamphlet on the beauties of Carolina. It is for William Hilton that Hilton Head Island, on Port Royal Sound, is named.

Hilton's pamphlet helped convince the Proprietors that money would be well spent on the colony. In 1669 each of them contributed 500 pounds sterling and agreed to pay 200 more each year for the next four years to establish a settlement at Port Royal, the site of Ribaut's colony. Each adult male settler was to receive 150 acres of land free; each female and each male under 16 would receive 100 acres. At last colonists began to volunteer.

The Proprietors put Joseph West in command of three ships carrying ninety-two passengers. The plan was to sail for Carolina by way of Barbados, where they would pick up more colonists who wanted to leave the crowded conditions of the island. In Barbados they replaced one of the original ships, which had sunk shortly after arrival, with a Barbadian sloop and welcomed aboard Sir John Yeamans, a planter commissioned by the Proprietors to be governor of the new Carolina colony.

On the voyage to the coast, the colonists ran into a terrible storm. The Barbadian sloop was blown clear to Virginia, another ship was wrecked in the Bahamas, and the ship *Caroline*, with Yeamans aboard, was blown to Bermuda.

When Yeamans reached Bermuda safely, he began to have second thoughts about the Carolina colony. Sending Bermuda's eighty-year-old governor, William Sayle, in his place, he returned to Barbados.

In April 1670, the *Caroline* finally reached Sewee Bay instead of Port Royal as originally planned. The Indians there were friendly and hospitable, and a visiting chief, the Casique of Kiawah, hoping for protection against the Spaniards and their Indian allies, the Westoes, talked the colonists into settling in his tribe's area. This was on the west bank of the Kiawah River, now known as the Ashley, where Town Creek joins the river. Soon the Barbadian sloop that had been blown to Virginia showed up to join the party, and Charles Town began to take form.

Accompanying the original colonists was Dr. Henry Woodward, a character whose real-life adventures rivaled the wildest fiction. A surgeon from Barbados, Woodward had gone on a voyage of exploration along the Carolina coast four years earlier, with Robert Sandford from the Cape Fear settlement. Woodward had asked to be left ashore to learn the ways of the Indians. He had made friends with the natives of the Port Royal area and had been adopted into the tribe, learning their language and studying their ways. But when the Spaniards heard that an Englishman was living in what they considered their land, they sent an expedition to capture Woodward and take him to St. Augustine, where he was put in prison.

As luck would have it, an English buccaneer, Robert Searle, happened to attack and capture the town of St. Augustine, releasing all prisoners and taking along those who wanted to join the crew.

Since a surgeon was more in demand aboard ship than anyone except a carpenter, Woodward was able to sail the Spanish Main until the ship was wrecked in a hurricane. He was cast ashore on the island of Nevis, where he was picked up by the *Caroline* on the way to settle Charles Town.

During the colony's first few months, the settlers depended upon Woodward's help as a physician and interpreter, as well as his knowledge of planting and building methods in the New World. His Indian friends warned them of attack and helped fight the hostile tribes sent against them by the Spaniards. Woodward's trips to the interior blazed trails which would become the basis of a trade in furs and hides—a main source of revenue for early Carolina.

Now that a real start had been made in Carolina, colonists began to flock to the little town which, after ten years, had been moved from Albemarle Point to Oyster Point, between the Ashley and Cooper rivers (both named for Lord Ashley-Cooper). The colony's guarantee of religious freedom brought Quakers and Huguenots, Lutherans and English Dissenters, even Jews. Rich and poor, criminals and honest citizens, tradesmen and aristocrats were given land inside and outside the walled town. Those unable to pay for passage across the ocean became bond servants, selling their labor for a fixed number of years to wealthier colonists who paid their passage.

In the beginning, Charles Town resembled the cities of Europe in the Middle Ages. Citizens were given lots inside the town walls on which to build homes and fields outside the walls in which to grow crops. The town faced the Cooper River and was protected on its land sides by a palisade. Gates were closed at sundown, and anyone outside had to identify himself to a sentry. The gates were set in bastions named for the Proprietors, and some had devices called "half moons" that swung around, closing an inner gate as the outer gate opened; these would let only one person in at a time.

Because the town had been planned before it was moved from Albemarle Point, Charles Town's streets were laid out by a surveyor and were wide enough to allow carriages to pass. Along the waterfront, docks—called "bridges" by the townspeople—soon reached out into the river. Marshes covered what is now the Battery, and creeks ran through parts of the town. Ships from Europe anchored offshore or warped in to the docks, bringing more and more settlers.

As first, the colonists had small ten-acre plots outside the city on which they grew food for their tables and planted the experimental crops ordered by the Proprietors: oranges, lemons, limes, pomegranates, figs, wheat, potatoes, flax and tobacco. Mulberry trees were planted with the idea of raising silkworms, which feed on their leaves; cotton and sugar cane were favored by the Barbadians.

When the fields near town had all been allotted, the colonists began spreading their acreage out along the banks of the Ashley and Cooper rivers and along Goose Creek, which empties into the Cooper north of town. Most of them had houses in town in case of Indian raids, but also built cottages like the ones in Barbados on their plantations. Unlike New England, where small, compact villages grew up, Carolina had only one town, Charles Town, with

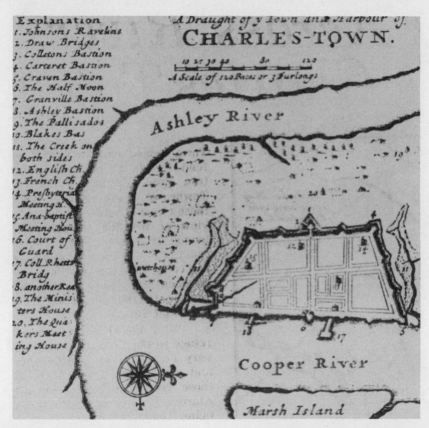

From a Herman Moll map, 1715. Photograph courtesy of Columbia Newspapers, W.D. Workman.

plantations spread out along the rivers and boats used more often than horses to get from place to place.

Almost from the beginning, the Barbadians ran Carolina society and government. Sir John Yeamans finally came to Charles Town in 1671, shortly after Governor Sayle died, to take over the governorship from Joseph West, whom Sayle had named as his replacement. With him, Yeamans brought slaves from his Barbados plantation.

Other planters, like Yeamans, came well supplied with wealth and property, and with the knowledge of plantation management. Their English-style society, formed in Barbados, was transplanted to Carolina, with all the provincial snobbery found in isolated posts of empire.

The Huguenots had lived for years in England and had adopted English language and ways; many of them were artisans and craftsmen. Their French names had been twisted around English tongues until they were hardly recognizable. A few had aristocratic backgrounds, and most were intelligent, adaptable, hard-working citizens who soon made their own niche on a high level of the Carolina social and political scale. The wrought iron of Huguenot craftsmen and the architecture of Barbadian planters combined to form Charles Town homes.

The letters of one Huguenot settler, Judith Manigault, tell of the hardships they endured. Writing to her brother, she relates how her family left France in the night to escape the soldiers quartered in their house. Forced to abandon all their belongings, they traveled to England by way of Holland, then joined a company of colonists sailing for Carolina in 1685. During the journey, which took nine months, her mother died of smallpox. The ship was so badly damaged in a storm that it had to put in to Bermuda, where the captain was imprisoned and the vessel seized. With very little money left, Judith, her husband and an older brother found passage on another ship and arrived in Carolina poverty-stricken. Accepting the land that was given them and working like slaves, they were hardly able to scratch out a living. Then her brother, weakened by the unaccustomed labor, died of a fever, leaving Judith and her husband to struggle along.

"Since leaving France," she writes, "we had experienced every kind of affliction—disease—famine—pestilence—poverty—hard labor. I have been for six months together without tasting bread, working the ground like a slave. . . . God has done great things for us, enabling us to bear up under so many trials."

Like many other Huguenots who were accustomed to the good things in life but willing to give them up in order to worship as they chose, Judith Manigault was able to conquer the wilderness and leave a heritage to her children. Her son Gabriel Manigault inherited the property and became one of the three richest men in America; he eventually gave $200,000 to support the American Revolution.

Although most early colonists lived and worked on the land, Charles Town was the center of social and political life for the people who gathered from outlying plantations. Beyond the reaches of the riverbank plantations, however, were hundreds of miles peopled by Indians. Henry Woodward had explored their haunts and brought back accounts of fertile lands, forests filled with game and streams teeming with fish. The Proprietors hoped to start a profitable trade in furs, and Woodward made treaties of friendship with the tribes of the backwoods, encouraging them to help the English against the Spaniards. Indian paths became highways along which thousands of pelts were brought to the port to be shipped to England. Along the paths and in Indian towns, freedom-loving English and Scotch-Irish yeomen set up stores and trading posts to gather in furs for transport to the sea.

Since the crops planted by the colonists brought little income to the Proprietors, the fur trade was the best source of return on their investment. To insure a prosperous trade, Lord Shaftesbury drafted laws for traders to follow to keep them from stirring up trouble among the Indians: Friendly natives were not to be enslaved. Fair payment was to be given for pelts. To oversee the trade and make sure the Proprietors received a fair share of the profits, Henry Woodward was sent as an Indian agent.

It was also Woodward who, according to legend, introduced Carolina to the crop that, together with Indian trade, would make the colony prosper for 150 years. A New England sea captain named John Thurber, just back from Madagascar, is said to have given Woodward a sack of the golden seed rice which was so successfully cultivated by the natives of that island. Woodward supposedly planted and cultivated the rice in a plot inside the walls of the town, with creek water used to flood the plants after they sprouted and from time to time during the growing season. The crop was successful, and seed rice was distributed to friends with plantations along the rivers. Within a few years, rice had overshadowed furs as a source of revenue.

But during the early years, before the planting of rice, the Indian trade was a sure and speedy avenue to wealth. The Proprietors tried to close the trade to private individuals, for fear that greedy traders would anger the Indians and because they were looking for fortunes themselves. Trade was limited to agents licensed by the governor. Soon trouble was brewing between the colonists and the Proprietors. Many of the colonists were in debt to the Proprietors and were dissatisfied with the distribution of land. Most of all, they were squabbling over the Indian trade, with some backwoodsmen enslaving Indians in spite of the law and colonists buying and selling furs illegally, short-changing both Indians and Proprietors. In Europe as well as the Indies, land meant prestige, and Carolinians invested in land as they made money in trade. In 1683 Lord Shaftesbury died. Three years later, Henry Woodward died, leaving no one who was particularly interested in regulating the Indian trade.

All through the 1680s, more colonists flocked to Carolina, most of them settling near Charles Town. Some, like the Scots led by Lord Cardross, did attempt to found a new colony. In 1684 these Highlanders were given a grant to land near present-day Beaufort. They named their settlement Stuart's Town and, since the Scots were famous as fighters, it was hoped they would serve as a first line of defense against Spanish Florida. But in 1686 the Spaniards swarmed over the town in a surprise attack; to complete the devastation, a hurricane struck, destroying the town and causing both Scots and Spaniards to abandon the site.

In 1697 a group of 158 Puritans from Dorchester, Massachusetts, established a town of the same name on the Ashley River above Charles Town. The Puritans held on for fifty years. Then, perhaps because they disapproved of the frivolity and worldliness of Charles Town, they moved on to settle what later became Liberty County, Georgia.

The "gentry" of Carolina arose from the original Barbadian planters and the Huguenots, who were soon able to establish fortunes by their industry and knowledge. A sort of plutocracy evolved, based on acquired wealth and land rather than "noble" birth. Locke's fundamental Constitutions were not for Carolinians. Religious and political freedom, yes! But a feudal system was centuries out of date. The system of landgraves, caciques and leetmen never caught on in the colony. Nobody wanted to be a leetman! The Carolinians were independent-minded and chafed under regulation by outsiders. Even though the Proprietors had paid for the colonial venture and were supposed to have power over the colonists, they were never able to enforce their laws. Carolina merchants and planters were a law unto themselves.

By the early 1690s, the success of the rice growers had led to the swelling of the slave population. Governor Nathaniel Johnson alone imported over 100 blacks to work in his rice fields. White colonists and Indians sickened and died in the mosquito-laden air of the rice

Field hands standing in a flat boat containing rice. Photograph courtesy of South Caroliniana Library, University of South Carolina.

fields, but blacks seemed to be able to stand the labor and remain healthy. In the sugar islands, the life expectancy of a slave after he was sent to the fields was about six years. Better treated in Carolina, they thrived and multiplied. Within a few years of the introduction of slavery, ships laden with hundreds of pounds of rice sailed out of Charles Town, bound for the Indies, the northern colonies and Europe; they returned with holds full of valuable trade goods. Ships loaded with black slaves arrived from Barbados and Africa, bringing workers for the rice fields. Uncivilized by European standards, unable to understand or speak English coherently, these blacks were bought by Carolinians as they would buy mules or oxen to work on their plantations. As valuable property, they were fed and clothed and kept healthy. But they were not regarded as members of society.

Although Locke's feudal nobility plan had not caught on, Carolinians early established their own aristocracy based on wealth and land. City-dwelling merchants had plantation lands, and those who based their fortunes on rice culture had homes in town for the social season.

The Barbadians, most of whom had plantations on the banks of the Santee and along Goose Creek, were staunch Church of England men and resented the influx of other religious groups into the colony. As they dominated social and political life, they also tried to dominate the financial life of the colony. Engaged in the Indian trade, trafficking with the smugglers and pirates who infested the coast, they resented the Proprietors' efforts to regulate the Indian traders and suppress the pirates.

In 1678, a Quaker named John Archdale had bought John Berkeley's proprietary share for his infant son. Finding Carolina split into factions according to religious, political and financial interests, he was determined to lessen the friction in government for the sake of his investment. Archdale had himself appointed governor and plunged into the task of reform.

The Archdale Laws, as his reforms were called, regulated colonial life so that much of the bickering stopped. The old Fundamental Constitutions were done away with completely, and the Governor's Council was replaced by an Assembly consisting of an appointed Council and an elected Commons House, with the Commons House having the deciding voice.

One statute declared that these Archdale Laws could not be

changed, even by the Proprietors, without the consent of the Assembly. Laws regulated the price of land and the collection of rents, with a portion of rents going to pay the governor's salary. Liquor sales and tavern operation came under regulation, and money was provided for the poor. Marriages, births and deaths were to be registered, and the sale of whiskey to Indians was prohibited. All "aliens" were given civil rights equal to those of Englishmen, and religious freedom was guaranteed to all Christians except Roman Catholics.

The first comprehensive slave code was enacted under Archdale's leadership in 1696. In contrast to the liberal rights granted to all free men, this code provided legal sanction for the complete control of owners over slaves, with vicious physical punishment for any disobedience. Barbadians remembered slave rebellions in the sugar islands, and they were determined to maintain control in Carolina.

The Archdale Laws and the growing success of trade kept Charles Town busy, wealthy and peaceful for the next few years. But by the beginning of the 1700s, Carolinians were bickering again.

With religious tolerance encouraging immigration, Presbyterians, Anabaptists, Quakers and Congregationalists (as Puritans now were called) had begun to outnumber members of the Church of England. Finding land along the rivers scarce, these new colonists settled southwest of the city along the trading paths. With the Indians at their back doors, they were worried for fear traders would stir up trouble. The merchants, mostly Huguenots and Church of England men, backed the traders in getting as much for their money as possible, even if this meant short-changing the Indians. The argument created a rift between Churchmen and Dissenters, although religion had little to do with the problem. It was really a split between backwoodsmen and merchant-planters. In those days the backwoods began only a short distance from Charles Town, but the enmity begun at that time between Up-Country Scotch-Irish and English-French Charlestonians has never been totally overcome.

One of the backwoods Scots, Thomas Nairne, was a planter and an Indian trader, and he saw the importance of keeping the Indians as allies—not only for trade, but also for protection against the Spanish in Florida and the French, who were exploring and colonizing along the Mississippi. Nairne went on two expeditions led by

Governor James Moore, in 1702 and 1704, against the Spaniards in Florida with the help of a large band of friendly Indians. In 1707, the governor appointed Nairne Colonial Indian Agent, to keep peace along the trading paths. Since the Proprietors were neither enforcing the trading laws nor providing protection against the Spanish, Nairne urged the Assembly to turn to the king for help.

Nathaniel Johnson, who had succeeded James Moore as governor, was a merchant-planter who depended upon the Indian trade for most of his fortune; so did his son-in-law, Thomas Broughton. While in the Mississippi territory promoting an alliance with the Choctaws, Nairne found evidence that Johnson and Broughton were violating the laws against cheating and enslaving Indians. His report to the Proprietors resulted in Johnson's being removed from office.

But the harm had already been done. Indians who had at first been friendly to the colonists were turning hostile, and the French were doing their best to egg them on. Along the coast of North Carolina, the Tuscaroras went on the warpath, massacring over 200 colonists in the New Bern area. Two expeditions were sent to North Carolina from Charles Town to punish the Indians. The first group, mainly composed of Carolina militiamen, was led by John Barnwell, thenceforth known as "Tuscarora Jack." The other group, composed mainly of friendly Yemassees, was led by Colonel James Moore, Jr. The Tuscaroras were so badly defeated that they left the Carolinas and migrated north to join the Iroquois Confederacy.

Peace, however, did not last very long. In the mountains of western Carolina, Price Hughes, a friend of Nairne, was making treaties with the Cherokees, establishing trading posts in what is now Alabama, and encouraging them to keep the French-led Choctaws from attacking English traders. But on his way back to Charles Town, Hughes was killed by Tohome Indians who were angry over English slave raids.

Nearer home the Yemassees, who had been friendly to the colonists, had grown tired of mistreatment. Thomas Nairne had worked for their welfare as Indian agent. Warned that the Yemassees were about to attack Charles Town because they were tired of cheating and enslavement by Carolina traders, Nairne went to a Yemassee town and tried to dissuade them. Instead of listening to him, the Indians who had been Nairne's friends tortured him to death, then attacked the outlying plantations.

Governor Craven, fearing that all the Indians would unite to wipe out the colony, hurried to fortify Charles Town. The militia was called up, under the leadership of Barnwell, Moore and other experienced Indian fighters. North Carolina sent militia companies, and Virginia sent supplies. Negro slaves were armed and organized into battalions to help defend the colony. Settlers from the backwoods hurried to the city for protection.

To help the Yemassees came the Creeks, the Catawbas and other eastern Indians tribes. The Cherokees, who always opposed the Creeks, promised help to the English. Governor Craven sent Colonel Maurice Moore into the mountains to persuade them to fight, but they preferred to remain neutral, and the help never materialized.

For a year and a half the colony was torn by terrible slaughter on both sides. In the long run, however, the colonists were too strong and their weapons far superior, while the Indians' ranks had been decimated by disease. European diseases, to which the Indians had no immunity, killed far more natives than English guns.

Finally the Yemassees sneaked away to Florida to join the Spaniards, while the Creeks retreated beyond the Savannah. The Catawbas and other river Indians buried the war hatchet and settled down in their haunts along the Santee and Pee Dee watersheds, where they became dependent on the colonists' bounty and never fought against them again.

In 1717, to prevent another uprising, the Assembly sent soldiers to build and man forts in outlying districts. These were intended to keep watch over the Indians and to serve as a refuge for traders and settlers in case of trouble. Fort Moore was built on the Savannah near modern North Augusta; Congaree Fort near modern Columbia, where Congaree Creek and the Congaree River join; Palachacolas Fort on the lower Savannah; and Fort Beaufort on Port Royal Sound. John Barnwell went to London to recommend the building of a ring of forts from the Altamaha up into Cherokee country, to encourage the settlement of the Up Country. The colony was finally at peace—except in the west, in what is now Alabama, where the French and Spanish were still stirring up tribes against English settlers. Carolinians could get back to basics: the growing and harvesting of rice and the collecting of furs and hides, which were making colonials rich. The Proprietors (a whole new lot since the start of the venture) were cashing in on their investment without having paid any attention to the Assembly's pleas for help against the Indians.

5

The Pirates

France and Spain were no longer at war with England. The Treaty of Utrecht in 1713 had ended the War of the Spanish Succession—or Queen Anne's War, as it was known in the colonies. The Indians were quiet and now, for the first time since the Colony began, English ships would not be attacked by Spaniards. One report shows 587,465 deerskins shipped to Europe between 1706 and 1715. Barrels of rice by the hundreds were put aboard ships for Europe and the Indies. Furniture, fine rugs, damask, porcelain, silver and crystal were shipped back to furnish the townhouses of plantation owners and merchants of Charles Town.

But the peace that followed the Treaty of Utrecht had put a lot of seamen out of work. The Royal Navy of England was cut to the bone, and sailors who had fought for their country during thirty years of war now found themselves on the beach. When letters of marque were cancelled for privateers, the enterprising now went "On the Account" and became pirates; former navy men flocked to sign aboard or "requisition" ships of their own.

With the coming of peace, England was able to think about policing the islands of the West Indies, where she had allowed the pirates to stay as a protection against the Spaniards. Woodes Rogers, a former privateer, was sent with three navy ships to Nassau, the center of pirate operations, to offer pardon to any who would pledge to become law-abiding citizens. Hundreds took the King's Pardon, and some few kept the pledge.. Others returned to piracy but changed their base of operation from Nassau. Many sailed north.

The early colonists of Carolina had been happy to trade farm produce and fresh water for cut-rate supplies from occasional pirate ships that put into hidden coves along the coast. Few of the ships captured near Carolina held gold or jewels, and the pirates were glad to get rid of the farm implements and household goods desperately needed by the settlers. But as the number of "Brethren of the Coast" increased and colonial exports became more valuable, the situation changed. Pelts, rice and rum became prey for the Brotherhood, and those who had winked at the traffic in stolen goods before were now up in arms. The Lords Proprietors, however, would not risk more capital to send help. Carolina, both North and South, became the haunt of some of the most colorful and disreputable rogues in history.

Most famous, or infamous, of all the Brotherhood was Edward Teach, called Blackbeard. A great hell-roaring, hairy brute with a shaggy mane and huge black beard that sprouted just below his eyes and tangled with the thick pelt on his chest and shoulders, he was the terror of the coast from New England to the Spanish Main. Born in Bristol, England, Teach had sailed on English privateers until the war was over. Unemployed, he hijacked a slave ship, rechristened it *Queen Anne's Revenge*, and raised the Jolly Roger. He loved the limelight, and would braid lighted fuses into his beard before boarding a prize, so that he looked to his frightened victims like the Devil himself. Women were fascinated. His men were said to fear and hate him, but they followed him with a loyalty akin to love. When Teach left Nassau, he moved to North Carolina waters where, in cahoots with Governor Charles Eden, he preyed upon coastal shipping. When he was finally hunted down by a fleet of ships under the governor of Virginia, he fought to the death, firing pistol after pistol and roaring blasphemies until, with "twenty-five wounds, five of them by shot," he fell dead on the deck. The Virginians sailed to Bath Town with his head attached to their bowsprit.

Anne Bonny and Stede Bonnet were more closely connected with Charles Town—she at the beginning of her life and he at the end of his. Anne, the daughter of a Carolina planter, eloped with a pirate named Jim Bonny in defiance of her father's plan to marry her to an aristocrat. Finding Bonny beneath her standards, she left him to join Calico Jack Rackham's crew and become a pirate in her own right. After two years of harrassing coastal shipping and fighting all over the Caribbean, their ship was captured by the British. Anne was tried for piracy in Jamaica but, since she was expecting a baby, was allowed to await execution until after her delivery. It is known that Anne Bonny was never hanged, but history is silent about what became of her. Legend has it that she returned to the home of her planter father. There is no record of her maiden name.

Stede Bonnet also left a plantation for the life of a pirate. A wealthy and successful planter of Barbados, he had no need of more riches. Barbadians said it was to escape a shrewish wife that he fitted out a ship, hired a crew of rogues from the island's taverns, and raised the Jolly Roger. Knowing nothing of seamanship, Bonnet headed for Nassau, before the time of Woodes Rogers, to join the pirate community. Together, Blackbeard and Bonnet sailed for Charles Town, which had just lately been terrorized by another pirate, Charles Vane, and his crew. On the way, they captured several ships which they manned with pirate crews; by the time they reached Charles Town, they had an impressive fleet. Standing on and off Charles Town Bar for almost a week, they captured several outbound ships—among them one bound for England carrying Charles Town Councilman Wragge and his young son. The pirates held the council- man for ransom—which included a store of badly-needed medical supplies—and blockaded the port for several more days until their demands were met.

Bonnet returned to Nassau and took the King's pardon, but was soon sailing back to his old haunts under another name, as Captain Thomas. He was captured by William Rhett and taken prisoner to Charles Town, where he was treated with courtesy and housed in the Marshall's own home. After all, he was a Barbados gentleman, and probably kin to many of Charles Town's gentry. But when Bonnet was ungentlemanly enough to escape and set out to sea again, Charles Town could not forgive him. He was recaptured, and this time incarcerated like a common prisoner. Stede Bonnet was tried and hanged, his body gibbeted in the marshes that were later filled in to become the Battery.

With the pardons and the capture of Teach, Bonnet, Rackham and most of the other pirate leaders, the Brotherhood dwindled. Some settled down as respectable citizens, while some moved their operations south, along the Spanish Main; others became smugglers. Once again, without the help of the Proprietors, Charles Town had come through a period of danger.

Expansion Under
Royal Government

By 1718, the people of South Carolina had lost hope of any help from the Proprietors in solving their problems. Their pleas for aid in protecting themselves from the Indians had fallen on deaf ears, and now they had had to deal with the problem of pirates by themselves. When the Proprietors tried to change some of the laws made by the Carolina Assembly, Carolinians were furious. Appealing to the Board of Trade in London to take over the colony in the name of the king, they deposed Governor Robert Johnson, who was answerable to the Proprietors, and replaced him with James Moore, Jr., hero of the Tuscarora and Yemassee wars.

The Board of Trade, knowing the importance of Carolina to England, tactfully bought out the Proprietors' shares and sent a royal governor to rule the colony in the name of the king.

Carolina's first royal governor, Sir Francis Nicholson, had served as governor of New York, Virginia, Nova Scotia and Maryland before coming to South Carolina in 1721. Hot-tempered and set in his opinions, he made few friends. He rubbed the Scotch-Irish backwoodsmen the wrong way by his devotion to the Church of England and his attempts to keep "Dissenters" out of office.

By this time there were almost 20,000 people in South Carolina, and only a third of them were white. Most of the population lived near the coast, along tidal rivers and creeks where the water could be used in rice cultivation. In the backwoods, the Indians were becoming accustomed to white men's customs and were using tools, guns and household goods traded to them for furs. The Creeks, in the southwestern part of the colony, also traded with the French who were settling along the Mississippi. The Cherokees in the northwest traded with both English and French, but since their enemies, the Creeks, favored the French, the Cherokees favored the English.

English settlers kept coming, and many people from other countries began to settle in Carolina also. French Huguenots who had fled Switzerland to escape persecution now began to be interested in Carolina. Jean Pierre Purry, a Swiss from Neufchatel, promoted the development of a colony on the east side of the Savannah River, twenty-five miles from the sea. The English government granted Purry 12,000 acres if he would transport 600 Swiss Protestant colonists to his village of Purrysburg, where they were expected to start wine and silk industries. But the land was marshy, and many of the colonists died of malaria. The silk and wine industries failed, and most of the survivors moved to other parts of the colony. One of these Swiss Huguenots, Jeremiah Theus, moved to Charles Town and made a living painting portraits of Charles Town high society. His paintings provide a record of the clothes and customs of well-to-do colonists as well as preserving the likenesses of these early Carolinians.

The French Huguenots were not the only colonists to come from Switzerland. The English government was anxious to have hardworking colonists from any country to keep trade growing and revenue flowing into England. Pamphlets were sent to Germany and to the German section of Switzerland to encourage colonists for the townships that were being started in the Up Country. In 1735 German-Swiss began settling in the Orangeburgh township and in Saxe-Gotha township, near modern-day Lexington. Dutch Fork, between the Saluda and Congaree rivers, was named for the *Deutsch*, or German, people. Since they spoke little English, these settlers kept to themselves and formed their own society, worshiping in Lutheran churches.

In 1726 a group of Welshmen moved down from Delaware to found a Baptist community along the Pee Dee River, near Society Hill, in what became known as Welsh Neck. These colonists stayed to themselves to avoid religious squabbles.

Most of the backwoodsmen, aside from the original English, were Scots. Many of them had championed the cause of the Stuart line after George I became King of England. Banished to Northern Ireland, they had not prospered there, and many of them, known as Scotch-Irish, had emigrated to Pennsylvania and Virginia and had come down from there into the Carolinas. Other Scots had come directly from Scotland—those from the Lowlands often having enough capital to invest in land or business and become wealthy Low-Country merchants. But the Highland Scots usually came with little or no money, sometimes having to become bondsmen to pay for transportation across the sea. Driven from their "crofts," or small farms in Scotland when the landlords began raising sheep for wool manufacture, they had first moved to Ireland and then to America. Courageous, belligerent and freedom-loving but often uneducated, they spread out in the Up Country, drawn toward the hills and mountains that reminded them of their Highland home. The Lowland Scots were usually staunch Presbyterians, while the backwoods Highlanders were more likely to join Baptist and Pentacostal sects.

In 1743 the South Carolina Assembly passed an act that offered European settlers transportation to the frontier and furnished them with tools, livestock and a year's provisions. Each family received portions of salt pork, salt and corn to stock the larder, and each man received an axe and two hoes. For every five people, a crosscut saw, a cow and a calf were furnished.

In the backwoods, a man could find a plot of land that he liked, build a shelter for himself and his family, and clear land for a farm. When a crop was harvested (he had to prove his ability to farm), he could go to Charles Town to file a claim on the land. This was known as a "tomahawk claim," since the cabin was usually crudely built with a knife and tomahawk from timber cut out to clear the field. Many woodsmen laid several of these claims in succession, moving on until they found a fertile spot and leaving the previous cabin and field to be swallowed up by the forest.

After the first year on a claim, when the field was planted a second time, settlers found time to improve their rough cabins. Stones were brought from creeks to build fireplaces and chimneys, with clay used for mortar. Cracks between logs were filled with clay, and furniture was made by hand of hardwood, with seats of woven rushes or oaksplits. The first crude cabin usually became a kitchen or storehouse later, and another well-built cabin, connected to the old one by a covered walkway, was used for family living. Because of the connecting walkway, where dogs could take shelter in bad weather, this was known as a "dogtrot" cabin.

Early settlers in the backwoods were dependent on their own labor for their living needs. With roads few and rough, supplies had to be carried on horseback. Since there was very little cash in most households, trade was mainly by barter. When two or three families settled near each other, they swapped services and products. A blacksmith's forge or grist mill attracted settlement in the neighborhood. When a new family moved in, neighbors helped build their cabin and donated food and household goods. "Log rollings" and "house warmings" were attended by settlers from miles around. Wooden bowls and spoons, hand-made quilts and ticks stuffed with fir needles or goose feathers might be given or loaned until the family could make their own. There were few books in the back-

The Lawerence Corley Log Cabin, built in Lexington, 1772, is an example of an Up-Country dwelling. Photograph courtesy of Richard Taylor.

woods, but a Bible was brought in a saddlebag and kept in a place of honor even by those who could not read. The record of births, deaths and marriages in these old Bibles was often the only trace of a family's life.

Backwoodsmen wore buckskin hunting shirts and trousers and, when they could get them, wide-brimmed hats to protect them from the sun and rain. Fur hats were for winter. A long, hand-woven linen or linsey-woolsey (part linen and part wool) shirt served as both shirt and nightshirt. Deerskin moccasins or heavy boots of cowhide could be made during the winter.

The backwoods woman wore plain, serviceable clothing of linen or linsey-woolsey, spun and woven at home. (Very little cotton was grown, as it was too difficult to pick the seeds out by hand, but some farms kept a small patch for family use.) A shift came to the knees and could be worn as a nightgown or, with a long full skirt, as a blouse. Often, in hot weather, this shift was the frontier woman's only garment, and she went bare-legged and bare-footed in the house, or moccasin-shod in the fields.

Charlestonians in general had as little to do socially with the new arrivals as possible. They were conscientious, nevertheless, in helping them on their way west. Many of the "societies" that later became social clubs were originally founded by concerned Charlestonians to care for the Europeans marooned in the city on their way to settle the backwoods. The St. Andrew's Society, which helped needy Scots and their families, was founded in 1729; the St. George's Society, for English immigrants, in 1733; the South Carolina Society, for Huguenots, in 1737; the German Friendly Society in 1766; the Friendly Sons of St. Patrick (later the Hibernian Society) in 1774; and the Hebrew Orphan Society in 1791. Rather than have Charles Town filled with unemployed vagrants, as many of the Europeans might have become, the societies helped them on their way with advice and supplies, caring for them while they were in the city, and providing for orphans whose families had died on the way. When the tide of settlers subsided, the societies became the social clubs for Old Charlestonians that remain today.

Charles Town, by this time, was considered the most sophisticated city in North America, with social customs aping those of Georgian London. Ships from Europe crowded the harbor, bringing luxuries for the wealthy planters' and merchants' families as well as practical trade goods for Indians and backwoodsmen. England under the four kings George was famous for opulent living, and Charlestonians were determined to keep up with London fashions. Parties, concerts, balls and plays were held in the city. Fortunes were wagered on horse races, cockfights and card games, just as they were in London. Sons of Low-Country families studied in England at Oxford or Cambridge, many of them staying on to study law in the London Inns of Court. They returned with English clothes, English horses, English manners and English ideas of the good life. Their homes were filled with delicate mahogany furniture brought from England or copied by Carolina craftsmen from English designs. Their wives and sweethearts wore gowns and bonnets ordered from French and English modistes.

Although the thrifty, straight-laced backwoodsmen thought of Charles Town "ricebirds" as luxury-loving decadents, Charlestonians were builders of another sort from the Up-Country men. With manual labor performed by slaves, they were able to concentrate on building a cultured civilization in the New World. The Church of England, spurred on by the Society for the Propagation of the Gospel, built churches throughout the Low Country, their pulpits filled by earnest missionaries sent out from England. Church services were well attended, and slaves were provided with balconies so that they could go to the planters' church. A public library, one of the first in America, and a free school for the poor were supported by Charlestonians. Even a school for slaves was run by the Church.

Most Charles Town children and those of nearby plantations were tutored at home or went to small private schools run by clergymen. Manners, music, art and dancing were considered important, as well as the three R's. While older brothers left for England to finish their schooling, young girls learned the art of running a large household and managing a staff of servants.

While backwoodsmen were struggling to harvest small food crops, Low-Country planters were improving the culture of rice, which kept the colony rich, and experimenting with new income-producing crops. One horticulturalist who contributed much to the commercial success of Carolina was a sixteen-year-old girl, Eliza Lucas, who found a way to grow indigo plants in the Low Country and process the crop into blue dye. Eliza was left to run a 600-acre plantation by her father, a widowed British Army officer, when he had to return to duty in the West Indies. Experimenting with seeds which her father sent her from Antigua, she had one crop ruined by frost, and only a few of the seeds produced plants. Eliza kept trying different methods until, finally, she had a good enough crop to make into dye. A dyemaker sent from Antigua by her father showed her the complicated process of boiling plants and compressing the residue into small cakes of dye, and she taught the process to the slaves. The next year she distributed seeds among planter friends, so that Carolina was soon able to furnish dye to the English textile mills which had been buying from the French West Indies. With England and France at war again, Eliza Lucas had helped save the English textile industry and had provided a great new source of wealth for the colony. By 1747, 135,000 pounds of indigo dye were being produced, and it was not long before over a million pounds a year were being shipped.

Of course, Charles Town had many citizens who were not wealthy

An artist's drawing of an indigo press. Photograph courtesy of The South Carolina Department of Parks, Recreation and Tourism.

merchant-planters. There were always craftsmen and tradesmen: carpenters and cabinet markers, blacksmiths, livery stablemen, tavern keepers, chimney sweeps and others who catered to the needs of the gentry. Much of this work, however, was done by slaves. Slaveowners who had skilled craftsmen used them in their own homes and loaned or rented them to their friends. Many were allowed to buy their freedom with the money they earned. White craftsmen who came to Charles Town complained that they had to compete with black labor.

The life of slaves in Charles Town differed little from that of the white working class in European countries in the eighteenth century. White servants in England were put in service in wealthy homes by their parents when they were children, and were likely to stay on with the same employer all their lives, living in bleak attic quarters and being paid little beyond their room and board. Some were beaten by their masters or had their ears "boxed" for impudent behavior. Although technically free, they had little chance of finding other employment. English factory workers were paid so little that whole families, starting with small children, worked to bring enough home to stay alive. Farm workers lived at a bare subsistence level on land owned by wealthy landlords, where their ancestors had worked for generations.

Carolina slaveowners were carrying on a feudal system already established in Europe. As white workers were unable to stand the heat and fevers of rice plantations, black slaves were imported to do the work. But as the planters bought more and more blacks to work on their land, they began to be afraid that the slaves would rebel as they had on some of the West Indian islands. Although Carolina slaves were much better treated than sugar island slaves, the whole idea of keeping a strong, uneducated people in bondage made thinking men uneasy.

There was always the fear that, in case of an attack, the slaves would join the enemy or break loose and go wild. The Spaniards encouraged runaways to go to Florida, where they were organized into battalions to fight the English. In 1730 some of these escaped slaves from Florida started a revolt at Stono, near Johns Island. A plantation owner and his family were killed, and nearby plantations were burned, with the runaways trying to recruit slaves from those plantations. Before the revolt could spread, the rebels were captured while dancing around, drunk on stolen liquor. They were all executed except the slaves who had been forced to join against their will.

Except for this incident and the Denmark Vesey plot of almost a century later, there is little in Carolina history to show that slaves were rebellious. It is a tribute to black Carolinians, who outnumbered whites almost two to one, that they usually fought on the side of their white masters whenever Charles Town was in danger—during Indian uprisings, pirate attacks, the Revolutionary War, and even in the Civil War.

The whole idea of slavery was repugnant to many settlers of the backwoods, particularly the Scottish Calvinists. Reared in the belief that hard work and frugality were the ways to righteousness, they scorned the use of black slaves to do the work that should be the salvation of God-fearing men. To them the life of the merchant-planter class was full of indolence and sin. Backwoods settlers who owned slaves, and those were few, were often shunned by their neighbors. Most of them worked alongside their slaves, and kept the blacks in their homes until prosperous enough to build separate quarters. It was not until cotton became a profitable Up-Country crop, after the invention of the cotton gin, that the large black population spread beyond the Tidewater.

This cultural gap between the established, wealthy, slave-holding Low Country and the new, thrifty, hard-working Up Country eventually caused an enmity and distrust that lasted even after the colony was united in its struggle against English domination.

The Cherokee Troubles

In the early part of the eighteenth century, Up-Country settlements were widely scattered and easy prey to any Indian war parties that might decide to attack. Although the Creeks had made peace and returned to their villages after the uprising in 1717, they were constantly being pushed by the Spanish and French to attack English settlements. The Cherokees, enemies of the Creeks, professed friendship for the English, but even the Cherokees made isolated raids on Up-Country settlers.

In 1729 a Scottish baronet, Sir Alexander Cuming, came to Carolina to explore the Cherokee country, where he had once had visions of settling a large colony of Jewish refugees. Whether he still hoped to promote this scheme or whether he was just curious, Cuming headed upcountry in the company of George Chicken, the official Indian Commissioner. Leaving Chicken in the Congarees and going on to the capital of the Lower Cherokees, Keowee Town, Cuming found the Indians astir with rumors of French intrigue. He had no official standing and was deep in Indian territory with no reinforcements, but he strode into the Cherokee council house fully armed (against all Indian custom) and demanded that the Cherokees reaffirm their alliance with the Charles Town government. Just then a terrible thunderstorm hit the village, and the Indians, perhaps fearing the wrath of heaven, fell to their knees and drank toasts to King George. A crown of possum's hair, a few scalps and some eagle tails were presented to Cuming as tokens of esteem.

Taking advantage of their friendship, Cuming called a meeting of the councils of all the towns and initiated the crowning of an "emperor" of all the Cherokee Nation. Then, inviting two of the chiefs—Attakullakulla and Ketagusta—and five warriors to go with him to meet their sovereign, King George, he returned to Charles Town and sailed for London with his seven Cherokee friends. The Indians were dressed in English clothes and wined and dined by the cream of English society, and were assured by London officials that, when they returned to America, the English colonists would be prevented from settling near their towns. The Indians, in turn, promised to keep French and Spanish traders out and trade only with the English.

Sir Alexander Cuming, by his force of character and his innovative ideas, had advanced the settlement of the frontier. Attakullakulla and Ketagusta went back to the Cherokee Nation as friends of England and spent their lives trying to keep the English-Cherokee friendship alive. For the next twenty years, the Cherokees protected the Up Country from harassment by French, Spanish or hostile Indians.

With the Indians at peace, the frontier was pushed westward at a quickening pace. Governor Robert Johnson took office in 1730 (the year of the Cherokee visit to London) and implemented a plan which would subsidize the founding of townships in the Up Country by various European immigrant groups. These settlers would, hopefully, provide a defense of the Low Country against Indian raids in the future, and would bring in more white people without slaves to help balance the racial scale.

The backwoods had contributed to the colonial economy by sending furs and hides to the coast. Now there was a growing cattle trade. Up Country meadows were rich in grass and wild peavines, and cattle were taken to the backwoods to breed and fatten on the meadowlands. In the fall they were driven into pens, and some were slaughtered and their hides shipped to the seacoast; the rest were herded along Indian paths to the Low Country. Pigs, sheep, goats and turkeys—anything that could walk or waddle—were driven down from the hills behind the cattle, the drovers sleeping beside the paths with their flocks.

South Carolina rivers were too shallow for large ships and were full of shoals above the Fall Line. Goods could be transported in flatboats or canoes, however, from that point where the sand dunes had been in prehistoric days. Settlements grew up on the riverbanks at these points and where the drovers' paths crossed the streams at fords and ferries.

The influx of settlers to the backcountry began to worry the Cherokees. Land, according to their tradition, belonged to the Great Spirit and was only to be used by men as they needed it for crops. Game should only be killed on hunting lands to fill the need of the hunters. Now white men were building cabins and fencing in fields and forests, showing papers that said the land belonged to them. Indians were told to stay outside their fences and were not offered the hospitality of their cabins. Deer herds were being depleted. And some white men were living within the old Cherokee-Creek dividing line of Long Canes Creek.

The trade in deerskins had brought the Indians guns and ammunition, farm implements and clothing that they had never had before. Now they could not live without these things. White traders were supposed to give fair measure under Carolina law, but here they were so far from Charles Town that they could cheat the Indians unmercifully without fear of punishment. Attakullakulla asked Governor James Glen, who took office in 1743, to help; Glen was anxious to see the Indians well treated and tried to enforce the law. During the years of his governorship, he called councils of all the Creeks, Catawbas, Chickasaws and Cherokees and tried to make peace among them, and between the Indians and the English. An attempt was made to formalize the Long Canes Creek boundary of Cherokee lands. White traders were prosecuted for cheating. To protect the Cherokees from their enemies (and to protect the frontiersmen) Glen promised to build forts in Indian territory to be manned by Carolina militia. These militiamen would supervise trade, and all the Cherokee lands would be under the protection of the English king.

In 1753 Fort Prince George was built 100 yards east of the Keowee River near Keowee Town, the capital of the Lower Cherokees, at the northwestern end of the Cherokee Path and 300 miles from Charles Town. This fort now lies under Lake Keowee. Settlements along the way measured the distance from one end of the trail to the other. The town of Ninety-Six, near modern Greenwood, was never given any other name than its distance (ninety-six miles) southeast of Fort Prince George.

At this time, France and England were again at war in what was known in the American colonies as the French and Indian War. The Indians in the Ohio area, who were allied with the French, went on the warpath, killing and burning in English settlements. Overhill Cherokees, in what is now Tennessee, were being pressured to join the French cause. Governor Glen, by more council meetings and promises of protection, hoped to keep the whole Cherokee Nation loyal to England. He promised the Overhill tribes that a fort, Fort Loudoun, would be built to protect their capital of Chota.

At this touchy point in time, Glen was replaced by Governor William Henry Lyttleton, an aristocratic, scholarly politician who knew nothing of Indian affairs and had no respect for Indians as human beings. A succession of misunderstandings and acts of violence by both Cherokees and white men led to an Indian uprising that raged in the backwoods for more than a year, with scalpings and massacres and retaliatory raids until the whole frontier was on fire. The Calhoun family was attacked while fleeing from their settlement on the Cherokee side of Long Canes Creek, and Patrick Calhoun, then a boy, was one of the few to escape; he later returned to bury his mother and the rest of his family. Years later his son, John C. Calhoun, would become one of South Carolina's most famous statesmen.

In April 1760, Governor Lyttleton, who had finally ordered the building of Fort Loudoun after a needless delay, was made governor of Jamaica. Lieutenant Governor William Bull, Jr. took command—as he was to do many times in the years to come when inept governors gave up and left. The whole Cherokee Nation was now on the warpath, and the garrison at Fort Loudoun was cut off. At Bull's request, Colonel Archibald Montgomery and 1,200 British regulars joined the militia in a campaign from Fort Prince George across the mountains, burning Cherokee towns and leaving the whole Cherokee Nation on the verge of starvation. Unable to rebuild and replant before winter, the Cherokees gave up.

Bull had wanted to negotiate rather than destroy but had been overruled by the Assembly. Now he did his best to restore trade and keep the Cherokees from starving. In 1761 a treaty was signed that gave the English the right to build forts anywhere and prescribed the handling of outlaws. It also established a definite boundary for Cherokee lands, along the present Greenville-Spartanburg county line and then southwest to the east of present-day Anderson.

The
Regulators

The defeat of the Cherokees should have meant peace for the settlements of the backwoods, but danger now came from another quarter. During the Indian war, frontier families had gathered in fortified strongpoints when they were driven from their homes by fear of massacre. Known as forts, these refuge points were really houses or trading posts that had been surrounded by log palisades. Often they contained several buildings where families could crowd in for protection against hostile Indians. In times of danger, homes and fields were deserted and stock turned loose, while everyone hurried to safety. All able-bodied men were expected to serve in the militia of their district, to patrol the territory and defend the settlements. They were ordered to carry guns at all times, even in church. When they were away, their families stayed in the forts.

After the Cherokees were defeated, the settlers began moving out of the crowded forts and back to their homes, only to find that their houses had been vandalized, their stock stolen, their crops destroyed. In many cases, this was the work of lawless white men rather than hostile Indians. Vagrants found it easier to catch a stray horse or cow, or to clean out a deserted cabin of food and clothing, than to buy what they needed. Frontiersmen had always respected other people's property, but now the hospitality and honesty of the frontier were threatened.

As responsible militiamen and landowners left the forts to rebuild their farms and plant their crops, the ne'er-do-wells remained. Many women had lost their husbands and fathers and had no place else to go. Communities developed in the forts very much like the hippie communes of two centuries later, with morals thrown to the winds. Unwilling to go back to the labor of farming, malingerers from the forts began raiding farm settlements for food, livestock and money, and finally began kidnapping the farmers' wives and daughters. The forts had become outlaw strongholds.

Except for the militiamen, there were no real law enforcement officers in the Up Country. The only courts of law were in Charles Town, and criminals had to be taken there for trial—a journey of at least a week and often two weeks, with the likelihood of attack along the way.

The people of Charles Town were not interested in sending help to put down this backwoods crime wave. They had sent militia and ranger companies to fight the Cherokees; now let the backwoodsmen take care of their own rowdy element. Charles Town was more interested in the tax that had been levied by England, requiring

An artist's rendition of the Charleston waterfront around 1780. Photograph courtesy of South Carolina Historical Society.

stamps to be bought and placed on all legal documents, newspapers and such. Charlestonians refused to allow the stamps to be distributed, and they ignored the backwoods as they waited for the outcome of the Stamp Act crisis.

The farmers were in a terrible predicament. Finally, with the encouragement of a Church of England clergyman who had left Charles Town to preach in the backwoods, they organized their own resistance to the outlaws. Companies of determined farmers calling themselves Regulators were formed to break up the outlaw bands. At the same time, requests were sent to the Assembly in Charles Town for the establishment of courts of law in the Up Country, and for schools and orphanages for the children whose families had been broken up during the Cherokee War.

The journal of the Reverend Charles Woodmason paints a lurid picture of the backwoods at that time. Woodmason, who had come to Charles Town from England and had been active in politics and finance in the colony, was also a devout Church of England man. Shocked to find that there was not a single Anglican priest outside the Low Country, he studied for holy orders and went to London to be ordained by the Bishop of London as a Church of England priest. Then, moving to Pine Tree Hill (later known as Camden), he began preaching to the people of the backwoods. Despite the fact that he was afraid of horses, Woodmason rode thousands of miles a year on horseback, with a Bible, a Prayer Book and communion biscuits in his saddle bags, and a jug of communion wine tied to his saddle. Only ordained clergymen could perform marriages, and since they were few and far between in the backwoods, he spent much of his time marrying couples and baptizing their children. A narrow-minded curmudgeon, Woodmason nevertheless spent his life ministering to the "low people," as he called them, trying to improve their sinful ways.

The responsible Up Country farmers, though not necessarily Anglicans, respected Woodmason for his education as well as his religious zeal. They needed someone who could bring their troubles to the attention of the Charles Town politicians. Woodmason not only sympathized with their plight but also could write in a witty, sarcastic style that infuriated his victims while drawing attention to the problem. In the late 1760s the *Charles Town Gazette* carried Woodmason's letters, often under pen names, informing Low-

Country citizens of the bands of outlaws and the need for law enforcement. When his letters failed to get results, Woodmason sent a stinging petition to the Assembly, with a threat of attack by the aroused backwoodsmen unless a circuit court act was passed and help sent to put down the outlaws. This *Remonstrance*, as it was called, was backed by farmers whose family names are among the most respected in South Carolina today.

To Charles Town politicians, the backwoodsmen were uncouth, insolent trash. Instead of helping the Regulators, they sent out law officers to arrest them. Lieutenant Governor Bull did his best to bring Regulators and Assembly together but was stymied when a new Royal governor, Lord Greville Montagu, newly arrived from England, turned loose all the outlaws from the Charles Town jail as a gesture of good will. It took months of armed skirmishes between Regulators and law officers—while outlaws continued to kidnap and steal—before the Assembly decided to help the responsible backwoodsmen.

Finally, in November 1767, Governor Montagu asked the Assembly for help in the "unhappy situation of the Settlers" and the Assembly appropriated funds for the establishment of two Ranger companies to subdue the outlaws. (Rangers could "range" over provincial lines and would not have to stop at North Carolina and Virginia borders.) The Ranger companies—consisting mainly of Regulators, who were now able to operate legally—were formed immediately. By March 1768, the outlaws had been rounded up, many of them hanged, and the rest imprisoned. Those who escaped departed for Georgia or North Carolina.

During the next few years the Assembly passed laws establishing courts and jails in the Up Country parishes. By 1774 circuit courts were well established, with little courthouses and jails in Orangeburg, Ninety-Six, Camden and Long Bluff. If it had not been for the Revolutionary War, the Up Country would have been able to get on with its development.

Gathering
War Clouds

South Carolinians, like other colonists, had no idea of starting a revolution. They considered themselves to be Englishmen and loyal subjects of the king. Money from England had poured into the colony, first from the Proprietors and then from the Royal government, to encourage settlement and trade.

But South Carolina had become used to governing herself, as had the other colonies. Parliament and kings had struggled for power in England, had fought wars over religion and territory. Meanwhile, Carolinians had built a civilization in the wilderness and a trade empire to make themselves and England rich. Allowed to develop a parliamentary form of government, they had given more power to the elected Commons Assembly and less to the Council appointed by the governor. Royal governors came and went, but the Lieutenant Governor, a native Carolinian who could never be governor because he was not born in England, kept the reins of government most of the time.

Then George III came to the throne. The king's grandfather, George I, had become king of England in 1714, when Queen Anne, his cousin and the daughter of James II, died. The English had rejected the Roman Catholic Stuarts and, as the only Protestant cousin, George I was brought reluctantly from Germany to be king of England. He never learned the English language. His German-born son, George II, spoke broken English and left the governing to his prime minister while he led the English army on the continent in a war against France. But George III was English-born and determined to be a real king, to clean up government corruption and straighten out the finances of England.

The war that George II had fought in France, known as the French and Indian War in America, had cost England a great deal of money. Parliament decided that, since Americans had been saved from a takeover by the French, they could help pay for the war. In 1764, new customs duties were placed on such products imported from the Spanish, French and Dutch West Indies as sugar, molasses and wine. The next year a law was passed which required all newspapers, pamphlets and legal papers to carry stamps purchased from the British government. Parliament had not tried to tax the colonies in many years, and colonial assemblies had not been given a chance to vote on the new taxes. The stamps were printed in England and sent by ship to America.

The reaction was fast and furious, with protest meetings held from New England to Georgia. In Charles Town, the ship carrying the stamps was quietly turned away and its cargo never unloaded. But the people of Charles Town thought the stamps were somewhere in the city. Thinking the stamps were hidden in Henry Laurens' house, a mob broke in and ended up drunk on the wine from his cellar. Judge Shinner's house was attacked, but the judge served punch to the mob and they left.

Charlestonians were furious that their rights as Englishmen had been abused. Christopher Gadsden, a merchant and plantation owner who had become a leader of the artisans and skilled laborers known as "Sons of Liberty," was sent by the Commons House of Assembly to a meeting in New York, along with Thomas Lynch and John Rutledge. For the first time, Carolinians met with delegates from the other colonies as Americans rather than as Englishmen.

In England, some liberal-minded statesmen who were in favor of representative government stood up for the colonists. William Pitt was influential in persuading Parliament to repeal the Stamp Act, and Charlestonians were so grateful that they paid a thousand pounds to have a marble statue of him placed in their city.

But England's treasury was still bare. In 1767 a tariff was levied on certain articles imported from England, including paper, glass, lead and tea. Finally England removed the tariff on everything except tea. As a matter of principle, the angry colonists refused to buy tea.

The William Pitt statue in Charleston. Photograph courtesy of Wofford College.

The merchants cancelled their orders but the tea was shipped anyway. In Boston the ships carrying the taxed tea were boarded by colonists disguised as Indians and the tea dumped overboard. In Charles Town plans were made to do the same thing, but word reached the lieutenant governor, and the tea was quietly unloaded and stored under the Exchange Building.

When George III heard about the Boston "Tea Party," he was determined to punish the rebellious Massachusetts colonists. Parliament agreed. Four laws known as the Intolerable Acts were passed, closing the port of Boston to all trade and cancelling many of the Bostonians' rights as free men. Again Pitt and his friends tried to help the colonists, but King George had become so furious that there was no changing his mind. This was one of the first signs of the insanity that overtook him in later life.

Carolinians, knowing that they could be treated the same as Bostonians, began to hold mass protest meetings in Isaac Mazyck's pasture, under a giant oak known as the Liberty Tree. In July 1774, men gathered from all over the colony, including the backwoods, to elect delegates to a Continental Congress to be held in Philadelphia. Even conservative aristocrats attended this meeting. Colonel Charles Pinckney was made chairman of a committee that was to continue between general meetings; John Rutledge, Henry Middleton, Thomas Lynch, Christopher Gadsden and Edward Rutledge were sent to Philadelphia. These men all considered themselves loyal British subjects who were simply protesting against the treatment of their fellow colonists from Massachusetts.

In January 1775 a Provincial Committee was formed in Charles Town. Forty of the new committee's members were also members of the Commons House of Assembly, which could be dissolved by the governor. The responsible men of the colony wanted to be sure they had an organization to take control in case the Assembly was dissolved.

By April, it was clear that the king would not give in, and Charlestonians slipped in at night and seized the guns and powder from the government magazine. Lieutenant Governor Bull was in sympathy with the colonists, but he felt that as acting governor he had to follow orders from England. Bull knew that many members of the Commons House had been involved in the theft, but with a straight face he reported the theft to the Commons, and they replied that they were unable to obtain "certain intelligence" about it. Nothing more was done.

That same month, word came of fighting between British soldiers and colonists at Lexington and Concord, Massachusetts. The Provincial Congress of South Carolina met in May to assume power, raise troops, issue paper money and join the association of colonies to restrict trade with England. A new royal governor, Lord William Campbell, arrived with his wife (a Charlestonian) to take over the government. The Commons House of Assembly handed him a paper saying that they had appointed a new governing body. Then they adjourned.

The Council of Safety, headed by Henry Laurens, took over the job of running South Carolina. This group was composed of some moderates who believed that changes in policy short of a complete split with England were still possible. It also contained radicals who believed that revolution was the only answer to colonial problems. In the Low Country there were many more revolutionaries than there were moderates.

In the backwoods, the opposite was true. With thousands of Indians loyal to King George, frontiersmen were afraid of an uprising. Besides, they had no love for the Low-Country "ricebirds" and little sympathy with their complaints against the king. Backwoodsmen didn't use much paper or glass and drank little tea. German settlers sympathized with the Hanoverian King George. After being left to fight their own recent battles with the outlaws, former Regulators were not about to help the Low Countrymen against the king. The whole frontier wanted to settle down in peace.

Most responsible men of the backwoods were members of militia companies. In case of trouble, they could be called up like National Guard members today. Militiamen were paid by the royal government for the time they spent away from home, and powder and lead were stored in their armories to be used when needed. When orders came from the Council of Safety in Charles Town to seize this powder for the use of the rebellious Low-Country radicals (as the backwoodsmen thought of them) trouble began. Militiamen felt the powder belonged to the king and was to be used for protection against the Indians; they refused to release it.

William Henry Drayton, a young aristocrat from Charles Town who had studied law in London, was ready to fight for the rights of Americans according to English law. Like many of the younger generation, he thought it was time to form a separate government. In July 1775, Drayton and a Presbyterian minister, William Tennent, journeyed through the Up Country trying to convince settlers to join the rebellion. When backwoodsmen refused, Drayton encouraged their neighbors who favored revolution to punish the neighborhood Loyalists. As often happens, people who were stirred up by

William Henry Drayton. Photograph courtesy of South Caroliniana Library, University of South Carolina.

political disagreement forgot friendship and family loyalty and acted like outlaws. Houses were set afire, people were whipped and tortured. Many who would have liked to remain neutral and live in peace were turned against one another.

Thomas Brown, a wealthy Englishman from Yorkshire, had recently arrived in the Georgia backwoods near the Carolina border, bringing bondsmen with him to establish a farming community. Brown got into an argument in a tavern in Augusta. "Liberty Boys" who had been drinking with him turned savage and tried to make him change his politics. When he refused to renounce King George, they took him out and poured hot tar and feathers on him. When he still refused, they put his feet in the fire. Brown finally gave in and was left to find his way to friends in the Ninety-Six District of South Carolina. When he recovered from his burns, Brown became one of the king's most rabid supporters. He left for Florida, which had become an English colony, and was made an officer in the Loyalist forces. Like many other backwoodsmen, he was incensed by the treatment that Patriots gave to those who opposed their ideas.

On Drayton and Tennent's trip through the Up Country, the two Patriots ordered out militia companies and spoke to them about the troubles with the mother country, asking them to sign an Association under the Provincial Congress. In the eastern part of Carolina, they signed on hundreds of men. After crossing the Broad River, however, they found that the farther they went, the less enthusiastic were the settlers. The Germans in Saxe-Gotha refused to sign. They were grateful to the king for their land grants and afraid of losing them. When the two men reached the fort at Ninety-Six, Thomas Fletchall, in command of the militia, signed a treaty of neutrality, although the militiamen there were loyal to the king and wanted to fight. Two months later the Loyalists attacked the fort, now held by Major Andrew Williamson and his men, who were only lukewarm Patriots. This was the first blood to be shed in South Carolina over the question of loyalty to the king. The encounter ended in an armistice and an agreement that the Loyalists would stay north of the Saluda River.

The second clash came when word got out that Patrick Cunningham, a dedicated Loyalist, was trying to stir up the Cherokee Nation. Colonel Richard Richardson, from the high Hills of Santee, collected a force of 4,000 militiamen under orders from the Council of Safety and, in the "Great Snow Campaign" of November and December 1775, swept through the Up Country, capturing and disarming Loyalists with little opposition except along the Reedy River. By the first of January, Richardson released his prisoners and he and the militia went home to get ready for spring planting. The Loyalists settled down to be neutral for the next five years, until the British Regulars took over the backwoods.

Meanwhile, Low-Country Patriots had taken over the government. Governor William Campbell dissolved the Commons Assembly and fled aboard the British ship *Tamar* on September 15, 1775. The Provincial Congress, with most of its members from the House of Commons, was now in control. But when Christopher Gadsden came back from the Continental Congress in March 1776 and proposed that South Carolina declare herself independent of England, the Provincial Congress refused. South Carolina was still British, despite her dispute with the king.

Even in June 1776, when the Second Continental Congress met in Philadelphia to frame the Declaration of Independence, a final vote was delayed by Edward Rutledge of South Carolina until after the first of July. The whole South Carolina delegation voted "no" on the first vote, but changed their minds the next day, after hearing that Charles Town had been attacked.

When the Declaration was finally ready for signatures, four South Carolinians—Edward Rutledge, Thomas Heyward, Thomas Lynch, Jr. and Arthur Middleton—all signed without hesitation.

The Revolutionary War

By 1776 the Continental Army was scrambling to organize in the North. General George Washington of Virginia, a hero of the French and Indian War, was chosen Commander in Chief, and General Charles Lee of Virginia had been ordered to take over the troops that were being organized in South Carolina.

On June 10, 1776, the British Fleet, escorting transports full of British Regulars, arrived off Sullivan's Island at the entrance to Charles Town Harbor. On one side of the harbor entrance lay Fort Johnson, on James Island, ready to bombard ships trying to enter. On the other side, on Sullivan's Island, Carolinians under Colonel William Moultrie were hurrying to complete a fort.

Without time or conventional building materials, Moultrie had made the best of what he had. Using the island's plentiful palmetto trees to build his outer palisade and filling the cracks with sea sand, Moultrie had built the sides of the fort that faced the sea to withstand bombardment. The center of the fort was filled with sand, and barracks and gun emplacements were built around the edges, inside the palmetto wall. But the landward side of the fort was yet to be finished.

With the arrival of the fleet, it became certain that the fort could not be completed in time. General Lee thought it should be abandoned—but the Virginian knew nothing of palmettos or Carolinians. Colonel Moultrie and Lieutenant Francis Marion and their men chose to stay in the fort and fight. Colonel Thomson and a

An artist's drawing of the attack on Fort Moultrie on Sullivan's Island, June 28, 1776.

company of Rangers, with Lieutenant Thomas Sumter and his backcountry riflemen, were sent to the other end of Sullivan's Island to stop any British troops that might try to come ashore there.

Informed by spies that the fort was unfinished, the British planned to sail into the harbor on the Sullivan's Island side and bombard the incomplete part of the fort. They sent boatloads of troops, under General Clinton, to land on Long Island (now the Isle of Palms) with instructions to wade across the channel to Sullivan's Island. What the British didn't know was that the channel was seven feet deep.

The English troops on Long Island set up camp and sweltered in their woolen uniforms for almost three weeks, then were shot to pieces or drowned trying to wade across the channel. The British fleet intended to sail around to the open side of the fort but ran aground on a sand bar and had to bombard the finished side, while the fort's guns tore them to pieces. Their cannonballs bounced off the springy palmetto logs or buried themselves in the soft sand in the center. Moultrie and Marion directed the guns of the fort so well that their shots severely damaged the British ships, killing and wounding many sailors. The captain of the flagship was killed, the

Commodore of the Fleet wounded, Lord Cornwallis hit by a splinter, and Royal Governor, Lord William Campbell, mortally wounded.

Once during the assault on the fort the flag with the insignia of Moultrie's troops, a white crescent on a blue field, was shot from the flagpole. Sergeant William Jasper picked up the flag and tied it to a ramrod, then climbed up on the battlements, with cannon and musketballs flying around him, and placed it where it could be seen again by the British. The next year, a palmetto tree was added to the center of the flag in memory of the palmetto logs that had stopped the British cannonballs. This new ensign was adopted as the flag of South Carolina.

By five o'clock in the afternoon, the British had had enough. South Carolina casualties included twelve killed and twenty-five wounded. The British had 115 dead and sixty-five wounded. Their fleet stood away toward Five Fathom Hole, and their soldiers gave up trying to cross the channel. By August 2 the British had vanished, and South Carolina was safe from enemies who came by sea. The attack on their homeland, however, had convinced the South Carolina delegates to the Continental Congress that they should join the rest of the colonies in signing the Declaration of Independence.

While the British were being beaten back by Charlestonians, the Up Country was once more threatened with Indian war. John Stuart, the British Indian agent who for years had kept the Indians friendly to white men, had been denounced as a Loyalist and fled to Florida. A true friend of both Indians and settlers, he was caught in a bind. Knowing that the Indians would scalp *any* white man, Patriot and Loyalist alike, Stuart tried his best to keep the Indians neutral; but he was ordered by the British government to have the Creeks and Cherokees ready to attack the frontier. At the same time, word was sent to Alexander Cameron, an Indian agent on the Reedy River, to start the "red stick" of war passing among the tribes. When word came that the British were attacking Charles Town, the Indians swarmed over the frontiers of Georgia, Virginia and both Carolinas. As Stuart had warned, the Indians attacked all the white settlements, killing and burning where they could, trying to rid their hunting grounds of settlers.

Many families who had remained neutral now turned against the British for setting the Indians on the warpath. Major Andrew Williamson, in command of the regiment of Patriots at Ninety-Six, assembled all the militia he could muster. Even backwoodsmen who were known to be dedicated Loyalists volunteered to stop the uprising.

Alexander Cameron organized British agents, traders and Cherokees to attack Williamson at the Keowee River, then slipped away. With Captain Andrew Pickens and his militia, Williamson then marched into the Indian lands, burning villages and destroying crops. Such officers as Sumter, Hammond, Rutherford, Hampton and Neil—who would later become famous in battles against the British—joined the expedition. Their combined forces destroyed the Cherokee towns from Keowee through the Overhill towns, in a campaign that lasted almost a year. In May 1777 the Indians sued for peace and ceded to the Americans all land south of the Appalachian Mountains. That winter the Indians nearly starved, and for many years they were too weak to fight.

With Sir Henry Clinton and the British fleet back in the North and the Indians quiet in the West, South Carolina could breathe more easily. For the next three years most of the Loyalists lived quietly, anxious to avoid a fight with their liberal-minded neighbors until the British Army could head south again. The Carolina Patriots sent delegates to the Continental Congress in Philadelphia and officers and men to the Continental Army of General Washington. Most Carolinians, however, stayed on their farms to produce food for the army and drilled with the South Carolina militia in their spare time.

Now that they had decided to be independent, Carolina Patriots tried to force all the people to declare themselves against the King. Many Loyalists departed for British Florida and the West Indies. Thomas Brown and other South Carolina Loyalists organized troops in Florida to be ready to help the British when they returned. Meanwhile, the British, having been repulsed in the South, had turned all their efforts toward defeating George Washington and his armies in the North.

While General Clinton had been attacking Charles Town in June 1776, General Sir Richard Howe and his brother, Admiral Howe, had been preparing for an attack on New York City, which was held by General Washington. Although the Americans fought bravely, they were fighting seasoned British Army and Navy regulars. In September, Washington retreated to New Jersey and, the day after

Christmas, made his famous crossing of the Delaware River to defeat 1,000 Hessian soldiers who were "hung over" after their Christmas celebrations. Two days after New Year's Day, Washington went on to Princeton, New Jersey, where he again defeated a British force; then the Continental Army went into winter quarters at Valley Forge.

The British spent 1777 trying to capture the whole state of New York, but in October 1777 American forces under General Horatio Gates defeated General Burgoyne's troops near Saratoga, and the world learned that the Continentals were a power to be reckoned with. France made a treaty of alliance with the Americans, and Spain seemed to be leaning in the same direction. The French Navy would now help to break the British blockade.

In June 1778, in the battle of Monmouth, the Continental Army mauled the British Army as they were evacuating Philadelphia. The British, commanded by Sir Henry Clinton, looked toward the South once more, convinced that the Loyalists there would come to their aid.

In December 1778, Sir Archibald Campbell sailed southward to Savannah with a force of between two and three thousand men. American General Robert Howe (not to be confused with British General Sir William Howe), a French and Indian War hero, was sent by Congress to defend Savannah and knew little about fighting in Georgia swamps. Savannah fell almost immediately, and most of the upriver crossings followed suit. General Howe was replaced by General Benjamin Lincoln as commander of operations in the South. The next October (1779) the Americans under General Lincoln tried to recapture Savannah but were repulsed.

In the bloody battle of Spring Hill Redout, outside Savannah, Count Pulaski, a Polish general who had come to help America, was mortally wounded. As the Americans charged up the side of the steep fortification, Sergeant Jasper of the Second Carolina Regiment was killed while trying, as he had on Sullivan's Island, to rescue the flag. Of the more than 600 South Carolinians who charged up Spring Hill, 250 were lost. Their opponents, the Loyalists and Indians who shot so accurately, were commanded by Lieutenant Colonel Thomas Brown.

With almost half of his men killed or wounded, General Lincoln moved back to Charles Town. In February 1800, the British fleet again sailed for Charles Town. The Carolinians had completed their defenses for an attack from the sea, but this time the British troops landed thirty miles south of town and, crossing the Ashley, marched down Charleston Neck to cut off the city. General Lincoln and 6,000 troops fought until May 19 to break through the British troops under Cornwallis, but were finally forced to admit defeat.

General Lincoln surrendered an army of 5,500 men. Members of the militia were allowed to go home after promising never to take up arms against the king again. Governor Rutledge and a few others had escaped up the Santee River; officers and government officials who had not already fled the city were imprisoned or took an oath of allegiance to the king.

On May 25, Thomas Brown was ordered to occupy Augusta, the city where he had been tarred and feathered. As he had at Ninety-Six, General Williamson withdrew without firing a shot, leaving Brown to wreak his vengeance on the people of Augusta. Meanwhile, the British under Colonel Nisbet Balfour took Ninety-Six again without a fight. Troops were sent to establish British posts throughout the Up Country, so that British communications lines soon stretched all the way from Augusta through Ninety-Six, Camden and Rocky Mount to Georgetown, and from Cheraw through Charles Town to Savannah. All of Georgia and South Carolina seemed to be conquered.

At this time, however, the British made an important mistake. Instead of allowing South Carolinians to remain neutral, they insisted that all pledge allegiance to the king or be punished. Then, on May 29, at a settlement known as the Waxhaws, a British colonel of Dragoons, Banastre Tarleton, cut down a regiment of Virginia Continentals under Colonel Abraham Buford, after they had asked for quarter. Word of this massacre and other atrocities by British troops and Loyalists made the backwoodsmen angry enough to abandon their neutrality. All over the Up Country and in the swamps of the Santee and Pee Dee, countrymen began looking for ways to strike at the "Bloody Backs," as they called the British red-coated soldiers.

Some South Carolina officers had been able to escape into the woods and swamps, where they formed guerrilla bands to spy on and harrass British forces. Francis Marion, Thomas Sumter and Andrew Pickens, who knew the countryside and its people, could extract loyal service from the independent backwoodsmen who would not have stood for formal military discipline. Sometimes their bands would be three or four hundred strong and then, when they were no longer fighting, all but a handful would slip home to plow their fields or harvest their crops. The tales of these men, particularly Marion, are some of the most exciting and romantic of Revolutionary legends.

Francis Marion was an undersized Huguenot farm boy from the French Santee region, who joined the militia forces in the 1761 campaign against the Cherokees, fighting under Captain William Moultrie as a second lieutenant. At the siege of the palmetto fort on Sullivan's Island in 1776, he helped Colonel William Moultrie turn the British fleet and army away from South Carolina—this time as a major in command of the left wing of the fort.

During the successful siege of Charles Town by the British four years later, Marion was in the city but had broken his ankle the night before the surrender. He was taken across the harbor and on to his home at Pond Bluff, near Eutaw Springs, on a litter. As soon as he could mount a horse without help, Marion gathered some of his former militiamen and went to join General Gates' army. When Gates turned up his nose at the ragged militia band, Marion led his men back to the Santee swamps where they were joined by other legendary figures—the James brothers, the Horry brothers, the Postell brothers, Witherspoon, Conyers, Maham and McCottery— all from the Santee-Pee Dee region.

Marion was appointed brigadier general by Governor Rutledge, and soon Marion's Brigade was making the lives of the British soldiers miserable with forays out of their swampland hideouts to attack and procure supplies and ammunition for their operations.

Once, when Tarleton had been unsuccessful in tracking Marion and his men, he declared, "Let us go back, and we will soon find the gamecock, but as for this damned old fox, the devil himself could not catch him." So General Sumter became the "Gamecock," and General Marion became the "Swamp Fox." Their activities kept the British from taking complete control of South Carolina.

As these guerrilla bands grew, the British tried to force South Carolinians to join the Loyal militia companies or be treated as traitors. That was all that was needed to win more supporters for the Patriot cause.

In August 1780, Cornwallis decided to leave South Carolina—

General Francis Marion, known as the "Swamp Fox." Photograph courtesy of South Caroliniana Library, University of South Carolina.

where the people had not flocked to join his army as he had expected—and march through North Carolina and Virginia to join the British armies in the North. At the same time, Congress sent General Horatio Gates, the hero of Saratoga, with an American army to help South Carolina. The two forces came together by accident near Camden, at two o'clock on the morning of August

16, each trying to make a sneak attack on the other. Gates' troops, sick, poorly supplied and outnumbered, turned and ran. Baron DeKalb, a German nobleman who had volunteered to help the Patriots, was killed as he and his Maryland and Delaware Continentals stood and fought to the death. Gates, with his army in flight, ended up in Hillsborough with only 700 of his continentals and a few militia left out of over 3,000 men.

Cornwallis continued to move northward to Charlotte, sending Major Patrick Ferguson, a Scottish officer, with 1,100 Loyalist militia to enforce law and order in the Piedmont. Word had reached Cornwallis that a band of North Carolina mountain men under Colonel Isaac Shelby had ambushed a force of Loyalists on the Enoree. The mountain men, after defeating the Loyalists, had gone home to celebrate. The expedition had been mostly for the sake of adventure, and the mountaineers were ready to settle down to their fall planting.

Ferguson sent word that the mountaineers should join the British forces, or he would "march his army over the mountains, hang their leaders, and lay their country waste with fire and sword." When word reached Shelby, he started immediately for the horse races in the Watauga Settlement, where he knew that Colonel "Nolichucky Jack" Sevier and his militiamen would be gathered. The mountain men were full of whiskey and ready to fight. They sent word to Colonel William Campbell of Virginia and Colonel Joseph McDowell and his brother, Major Charles McDowell, of the the upper Catawba, and to Benjamin Cleveland from the Yadkin, then set off to meet Ferguson. Being frontiersmen, they could live off the land and travel fast, and they were provided with food and drink all along the way by settlers. Ferguson heard of their march and started toward Charlotte to get help from Cornwallis, but he was only as far as King's Mountain when the mountaineers caught up.

Ordering his men up the mountain, Ferguson established a defensive position around the top so that he could shoot down at the mountaineers. But the mountain men used the Indian tactic of encircling and closing in on the enemy, thus cutting the British off from escape. Their riflemen picked off Loyalists as they moved up the mountainside. Forty Americans were killed, while all 1,104 of the Loyalists were either killed or captured. Ferguson was one of those killed.

British General Charles Cornwallis. Photograph courtesy of South Caroliniana Library, University of South Carolina.

King's Mountain can be called a turning point in the war. It gave new hope to the Carolinians who had gone home to their farms, and militia companies under Sumter, Marion and other Up-Country officers began to fill up again. With a chance of victory for the Patriots, they were ready and willing to fight.

In December, General Nathaniel Greene was sent to replace General Gates. Greene was a Quaker but also a fighter and a soldier's soldier. He set to work to build an army of backwoodsmen, using tactics scorned by more orthodox generals. His strategy was to pull Cornwallis' army farther and farther away from the British base in Charles Town so Patriot forces could attack British supply lines.

Cornwallis moved from Charlotte back to Winnsboro, and Greene sent General Daniel Morgan to lure Cornwallis westward so that Greene could attack him from the rear. Cornwallis sent Tarleton and his Green Dragoons to stop Morgan. An old campaigner from the French and Indian War, Morgan knew how to manage the backwoods militia, who were devoted to him. He also was suffering from rheumatism, sciatica and hemorrhoids, and was tired of being in the saddle. Instead of retreating before the British Regulars, Morgan moved into Cowpens (a village where the drovers had built pens to gather stock for their drives). With him were Colonel Howard's and Colonel Washington's Continentals and Andrew Pickens' militia.

According to tradition, a nine-year-old boy overheard a conversation while hidden outside Tarleton's tent and brought word of the British plan of attack. The next day, Morgan's army outmaneuvered Tarleton and defeated his British Regulars. Over 900 of Tarleton's 1,100 men were killed or captured, though Tarleton himself escaped with 200 of his Dragoons. It was the first time that an American corps, including militia, had defeated British Regulars.

While Colonel Pickens was fighting at Cowpens, his home in Long Canes was burned at Cornwallis' orders and his wife and children were turned out in the cold January weather. A slave named Dick took the family into his cabin and fed and protected them.

Cornwallis now moved northward, toward Virginia, while General Greene moved from the east and General Morgan came from the west in order to stop him. They met in March at Guilford Courthouse. Although Morgan and Greene were not able to defeat Cornwallis' army, they turned him away from Virginia toward Wilmington, North Carolina, where he remained until the following October, when he was defeated by George Washington's army at Yorktown, Virginia.

When he departed South Carolina, Cornwallis left the Loyalist militia in charge of all but the area around Charles Town, which was held by British Regulars. With only Loyalist militia to fight, the Patriot militia took heart and began to recapture their lands. Francis Marion's militia and that of Henry Lee put pressure on the British posts of Fort Watson, Fort Motte and Fort Granby, along the Santee-Congaree-Saluda River system, and on Augusta and Georgetown, until they had all fallen into Patriot hands. Ninety-Six, the toughest Loyalist stronghold, held on through the summer. Then Lord Rawdon, arriving from Ireland with fresh troops, marched west to evacuate the besieged troops and lead them back to Charles Town.

The last armed clash of the war occurred at Eutaw Springs in August, when General Greene again tried to recapture Charles Town. He was repulsed as usual. (By now Greene was famous for losing battles but making the enemy retreat.) The British drew back into Charles Town.

Finally, on December 14, 1782, the British Army embarked from Christopher Gadsden's wharf in Charles Town, taking with them 4,000 South Carolinians who were still loyal to the king and preferred exile to life among the victorious Patriots. Many of these families took their slaves and all their possessions, settling on plantations in the West Indies. William Bull, although born in South Carolina, left his home to settle in England.

Governor John Matthews, who had been elected while the government was in exile in the backcountry, rode into Charles Town with General Greene and proclaimed the state of South Carolina to be free from British rule. A treaty signed at Paris in September 1783 formally ended the war. England recognized the independence of her former thirteen colonies as a new republic, the United States of America. The boundaries of the United States were extended west to the Mississippi River and north to the Great Lakes. Congress was to recommend restitution of confiscated Loyalist estates. (The states disregarded this recommendation.)

South Carolina was free and at peace, from the mountains to the sea, ready to build on her newly-acquired freedom.

11

The Cotton Kingdom

As the Revolutionary War ended, a whole new way of life was beginning in Carolina.

Many of the 4,000 Carolina Loyalists who left Charles Town with the British Army were wealthy, aristocratic planters and merchants who took their money and slaves with them, leaving the city in poor economic condition. The indigo planters had lost their English market for dye during the war, and their fields had been abandoned. The rice planters, without free trade in the West Indies, were losing money. A new crop was needed.

For years most farmers and planters had grown a little bit of cotton, along with their vegetables, to be used by families and servants. Cotton grew well in the warm climate, but it took so long to pick the seeds out of the white fluffy fibers that the job had to be done in the long winter months when there was little outdoor work to be done. Even after the seeds were separated, the fibers had to be combed out by working them, a handful at a time, between wire-bristled brushes. Finally the fibers were spun into thread with a spinning wheel and woven into rough cloth on a hand loom.

While America was fighting its war for freedom, three machines had been developed in England to make the wool industry more efficient: James Hargreaves' spinning jenny, Richard Arkwright's power-driven spinning machine, and the Reverend Edmund Cartwright's power loom. If only someone could devise a way to process cotton fibers so that they were ready for spinning, cotton could be grown in the South and sold to manufacturers in England and the North, where woolen mills were already in operation.

So Eli Whitney invented the cotton gin.

Whitney, who had just graduated from Yale, had been offered a job teaching school in Up-Country South Carolina. In 1792, on a voyage from New York to Savannah, he made friends with the widow of General Greene, who had been given Mulberry Grove, a plantation near Savannah, in gratitude for his leadership in the Revolutionary War. Whitney went to visit Mulberry Grove before going on to take over his teaching job and, while there, learned of the need for a machine to separate cotton fiber from seed. Fiddling around in the plantation workshop, he put together a contraption of revolving saws, wire brushes and combs that took the seeds out and left the cotton ready to spin. His invention changed the future of the South.

Some plantation owners in the Low Country began to plant some of their fields in cotton, using slave labor to hoe and plant and pick the crop. They found England and New England mills anxious to buy the ginned cotton. Up-Country farmers, learning that their land would grow cotton where it wouldn't grow rice, cleared forests

The cotton gin invented by Eli Whitney.

and plowed meadowlands until the whole state began to be white with cotton fields. Up-Country farmers were as rich as Low-Country planters now, and ready to buy more land.

In the beginning, farmers in the Up Country planted and picked the cotton by themselves or with the help of a few slaves. But as they bought more land, they needed more black labor for their fields. As more and more black Africans were brought into Charleston and other Southern ports, the price of prime fieldhands skyrocketed.

With cotton to transport from the Up Country to the sea, roads had to be built between towns; canals had to be dug to link rivers, so that boats and rafts could carry cotton to the docks. Eight large canals were dug around major obstructions on the Broad, Congaree, Saluda and Wateree rivers. But laborers were needed to dig. Slave owners refused to sell or rent their valuable slaves for the back-breaking work of canal digging. Instead, workers were brought over from famine-blighted Ireland, their passage paid by promoters who contracted with the canal-building companies to provide labor, and the laborers paid starvation wages. These Roman Catholic laborers brought their religion with them, and for the first time, Catholic churches were built in South Carolina. Strong, hard-working and adaptable, the "Shanty Irish" soon became "Lace Curtain Irish," with influence in the politics of every town where they settled.

At first cotton was shipped to Charleston or Savannah. In the port cities were cotton exchanges where bales were sold to "factors" (representatives of textile factories) from England or the North and were shipped by sea to their destination. It was not long, however, before small factories were being built in South Carolina on Up-Country rivers and canals, where the water could be used to turn wheels and run machines, thus saving the cost of shipment.

With the price of slaves becoming higher and higher, and their owners charging more and more to lease them, Up-Country mill owners found that it cost less to hire white "piney woods" families. Factory towns consisting of small wooden houses were built, the first one by William Gregg in Graniteville. The homes rented for sixteen to twenty-five dollars a year, and the company provided a school and a church building. Men were paid four to five dollars a week, women and children (as soon as the latter were able to work) three to four dollars a week—for twelve hours a day, six days a week. The mill ran a store where its workers could charge their groceries and household needs. The workers had to buy their own food and clothing, but they were allowed to plant gardens in the yards of their houses and could grow some of their own food, if they were not too tired after twelve hours in the mill. There was no promise that anyone would be taken care of if sick, injured or old as there is in modern factories. In many ways, mill hands were worse off than plantation slaves but, unlike slaves, they were free to work or quit.

In the thirty years after the Treaty of Paris, high society in South Carolina had stretched to include the new cotton aristocracy who now lived in mansions that looked down from the red clay hills to survey snowy fields full of black workers. The reign of King Cotton seemed to be the greatest blessing possible for the South and its people. There was, however, a dark side to the white, fluffy cloud that Southerners looked on with such pride.

With cotton as the state's only real money-maker, little attention was paid to any other industry. While the rest of the country was building every sort of factory and growing every sort of crop, South Carolinians put all their land and energy into cotton. Even textile mills were few compared to those of New England.

To cultivate and pick the cotton, many more thousands of black slaves were brought from Africa and the West Indies, until they outnumbered the white people of the state. These uneducated but physically strong black people were fed and clothed, kept healthy and cared for in their old age, but they were given no freedom of choice. If stirred up, they could be a threat to their white masters. Most plantation owners felt that they treated and controlled their own slaves well, but they all feared the masses of black laborers belonging to other people. Because of their fear, they made laws to keep slaves in line. This fear has shadowed all the politics of South Carolina for the last two centuries.

With laborers (both black and white) being paid so little, European immigrants avoided the South and settled where there was a chance for advancement in skilled trades. South Carolina became a one-crop, one-industry community composed mainly of white Anglo-Saxons and black Africans.

12

The Rise of
Political Parties

As cotton brought a new social climate, so freedom from English rule brought a new political age.

Although many of the poorer Carolinians had hopes of a real democracy where every free man's vote counted equally, it was soon evident that the Low-Country aristocracy would continue to rule South Carolina. When a delegation chosen by the Legislature was sent to Philadelphia to the Constitutional Convention in 1787, the four representatives were John Rutledge, Charles Cotesworth Pinckney, his cousin Charles Pinckney, and Pierce Butler. Three were lawyers and one a planter, all from the Low Country. All four were in favor of "an aristocratic republic, but not a monarchy." The Up-Country farmers and city mechanics had no representative in Philadelphia.

Because they were not represented, the people of the Up Country were suspicious of the Constitution and against its ratification. In 1788 it was ratified by a state constitutional convention whose members were also mainly Low-Country men. "The Gamecock," General Thomas Sumter—"one of the boldest and most reckless of Carolina's partisans"—had retired to his plantation before the end of the Revolution to nurse an old but unhealed wound. Now he transferred his fighting spirit from the army to politics.

Sumter was one of the loudest protesters against the Constitution. He and most other Up-Country politicians agreed with Thomas Jefferson that the old Articles of Confederation could be revised

General Thomas Sumter, known as the "Gamecock."
Photograph courtesy of Richard Taylor.

instead of writing a new Constitution. They opposed Alexander
Hamilton's efforts to strengthen the federal government, preferring
that the states remain in a loose confederation. Jefferson favored
the revolutionary government in France, while Hamilton was for
strong ties with England. Jefferson's party became known as the
Republicans (nothing to do with today's Republican Party), and
Hamilton's was known as the Federalist Party. Most Low-Country
politicians favored Hamilton.

One victory for the Up Country came in 1786, when its representatives pushed through legislation to move South Carolina's capital
to the center of the state, away from Charleston. Charles Town had
been given a municipal government in 1783; in 1785 it had been

incorporated and its name changed to "Charleston." Now the port city would lose its position as seat of the Legislature.

Many Up-Country politicians tried to get the capital moved to their counties. General Sumter offered to donate his land in Statesburg so that the capital could be like Rome, built on seven hills. A site was chosen, however, near old Fort Granby, where the Broad and Congaree rivers met, and the new city was named "Columbia." A wooden capitol building was erected at the corner of Assembly and Senate streets, named for the two houses of the Legislature.

In 1790 a Constitutional Convention met in the new capitol building to try to write a new state constitution that would be more democratic than the original one created by Low-Country legislators. Charles Pinckney, a devout Jeffersonian, had been elected governor and hoped to keep the Low Country from controlling the Legislature. The new constitution gave more delegates to the backwoods but still gave a majority to the coastal region.

In national politics, South Carolina was well represented. Thomas Pinckney was on the Federalist ticket for Vice President in 1796. Charles Cotesworth Pinckney was on the Federalist ticket for Vice President in 1800 and on the Presidential ticket in 1804 and 1808. John Rutledge, Ralph Izard, Dr. David Ramsay and others were active Federalists. Charles Pinckney, Edward Rutledge, Pierce Butler and Wade Hampton, like Thomas Sumter, were active Republicans. Although most Low-Country politicians were Federalists now, there were some who supported Jefferson. And with cotton spreading wealth and slaves to the Up Country, many planters from this region were Federalists. Politics was becoming more a matter of rich planter and poor worker than Up Country and Low Country.

In 1808 an amendment to the 1790 Constitution gave more representation to Up-Country election districts, removing control of the Legislature from Low-Country hands. But since the new cotton aristocracy ran politics in most of the backcountry, the Legislature remained in the hands of planters.

The Nullification
Controversy

The War of 1812 slowed the trade in cotton, and it made famous two native Carolinians who were to shape the destiny of the whole nation in years to come.

John C. Calhoun, one of a group of young United States congressmen known as "War Hawks," helped push Congress into declaring war on England. Alarmed by the recession caused by a slowdown in the cotton trade, Calhoun was even more worried because the British were stirring up the Indians in the lands of the Louisiana Purchase, which the United States had bought from France in 1803.

John C. Calhoun was the son of Patrick Calhoun, a Regulator and later a Colonial Assemblyman from the Long Canes area of Ninety-Six District. As a child, Patrick Calhoun had escaped an Indian massacre in which his mother and other members of their party had been killed. Although he died when John C. was only eleven, Patrick Calhoun had taught his son to mistrust Indians and to fight for political freedom.

Handsome, debonair and an inspired speaker, John C. Calhoun was elected to Congress at the age of twenty-nine. He and other Carolinians hoped the United States could take Canada away from England and that Florida (which England had returned to her ally, Spain) could be captured for the United States. Then the Indians would not have bases on the northern and southern borders of the country from which to attack frontier settlers.

When Congress declared war in 1812, another Carolinian from

The north entrance to the John C. Calhoun mansion on the campus of
Clemson University. Photograph courtesy of Clemson University.

the Waxhaws, Andrew Jackson, was ready with an army of 3,000
trained Tennessee militiamen, equipped and ready to fight.

Jackson had begun soldiering at the age of thirteen, during the
Revolutionary War. When Tarleton raided the Waxhaws, Jackson
and his older brothers had become militiamen to defend their home.
After the war, Jackson studied law, then moved to what is now
Tennessee, where he became well known as an Indian fighter and
a rough-and-tumble politician. When Tennessee became the sixteenth state to enter the Union, Jackson was sent to Washington
first as a congressman and then as a senator. He then returned to
Tennessee as a superior court justice and commander in chief of the
militia. In 1812, as a major general in the United States Army, Jackson
was sent to New Orleans, where he fought the last battle of the War
of 1812. According to the ballad, with the help of Jean Lafitte and
his pirates, Jackson defeated the British and "they began a-runnin'/
Down the Mississippi to the Gulf of Mexico." Although this battle
took place after a treaty had already been signed, it was gleefully
cheered as one of the few American victories in the war. General
Jackson was nicknamed "Old Hickory" for standing firm as a
hickory tree.

Except for some raids on coastal towns and islands, South Carolina was not a battleground in 1812. Florida and Canada, which the War Hawks in Congress had hoped to annex, remained Spanish and British respectively.

In 1818, with James Monroe in the Presidency and John C. Calhoun as Secretary of War, Old Hickory was put in command of an expedition against the Seminole Indians, who were on the warpath in Florida, raiding across the American border. Calhoun, under orders from the President, instructed Jackson to "adopt measures to terminate the conflict," and Old Hickory took him at his word. The army went into Florida after the Seminoles, seizing Pensacola from the Spanish and placing an American governor over western Florida. When Spain objected, she was told that she must either maintain order in Florida or cede it to the United States. Calhoun, afraid he might be blamed for the attack, had secretly worked to have Jackson reprimanded. But when Spain gave in and gave up all claim to Florida, Jackson was the hero of the hour. His fame would carry him, a few years later, into the Presidency, with John C. Calhoun as his Vice President.

But two such hard-headed politicians could never get along. Jackson—whose beloved wife Rachel remained a backwoods woman even in the White House, shunning social functions and smoking a corncob pipe in the privacy of their sitting room—was famous as a hard-living, quick-to-anger frontier fighter. Calhoun, though born on the frontier, had married a Low-Country lady, Floride Colhoun, and had been accepted in Charleston society. With his dark good looks, brilliant mind and Yale education, Calhoun seemed more aristocratic than some aristocrats. His life was full of contradictions.

During his early days in Congress, Calhoun hoped to encourage Massachusetts cotton mills to use more Southern cotton; he therefore supported Northern manufacturing interests by voting for a tariff on foreign-made products. Hoping to keep the Indians under control by fighting the British, he supported the war in 1812. As a frontiersman, he also hoped the federal government would pay for roads and canals in the new territories. This meant that he called for a liberal interpretation of the Constitution, because a strict interpretation made the states and territories responsible for their own improvements.

But as cotton lands expanded west and huge crops began to be a glut on the market, the price of cotton dropped. Calhoun had built a mansion on his cotton plantation at Fort Hill, and he and Floride entertained lavishly for planter society old and new. Their planter friends, unable to admit that a one-crop economy was making them poor, now blamed the tariff for ruining trade. By 1825 John C. Calhoun had become an enemy of the tariff he had helped to create. In 1828, however, a tariff act was passed in spite of his opposition.

As Vice President, Calhoun was in his glory. Although many of his ideas were conservative and pleased the aristocracy, his fight against the tariff also pleased frontiersmen who needed cheap manufactured goods. Even the New Englanders, who were in favor of the tariff, admired his brilliant oratory. (Hadn't he gone to Yale?) Calhoun looked like a shoo-in for the Presidency in the next election.

Then Old Hickory heard about Calhoun's attempt to have him reprimanded ten years before, and the fat was in the fire. The crowning blow came when Floride Calhoun turned up her aristo-cratic nose and refused to return the call of Peggy O'Neill Eaton, a former barmaid and sailor's widow who was now the wife of Jackson's old friend, Secretary of War, John Eaton. Floride even summoned a servant to show President Andrew Jackson out of her house when he came to protest.

The fight was on, with Calhoun now representing the conservative planters and Jackson the liberal-democratic West. Calhoun jumped wholeheartedly into the "Nullification" movement, claiming that a state could pull out of the Union and reject the laws it found distasteful.

At a Jefferson's birthday dinner in 1830, President Jackson stood facing Calhoun and made a toast: "The Union—it must be preserved!"

Calhoun, with eyes blazing, countered, "The Union! Next to our liberties, most dear!" In the minds of South Carolinians, that was the lighting of the fuse to the bomb that exploded thirty years later.

The controversy smoldered until 1832, when the South Carolina Nullification Convention declared the tariff of 1828 and another recently-passed tariff to be null and void. Carolina would trade as she pleased.

In answer, President Jackson prepared to send ships and troops to South Carolina. Unionists in the state, under the leadership of Joel Poinsett—doctor, lawyer, botanist and builder of bridges in the Carolinas, for whom the Poinsettia is named—launched a campaign to keep peace. Finally, under his guidance the Nullifiers could retreat without losing face.

The whole tempest settled back into its teapot for the time being, but the principle of nullification remained in the minds of its creators. The question of slavery, however, was becoming an even greater source of conflict between North and South. It was an emotional issue, guaranteed to arouse sentiment in either region, and useful in forwarding political causes.

Most of the manufacturing states in the North had abolished slavery and fought to keep the territories free of slavery. An early act of Congress had forbidden the importation of slaves after 1808. (South Carolina had stopped its foreign slave trade in 1787, before the invention of the cotton gin, but had reopened it in 1804 to beat the deadline and secure more slaves for the cotton fields.) After 1808, smugglers continued to bring in slaves from Africa and the West Indies, much as illegal aliens are brought in to pick crops today.

Propagandists in the North stirred hatred and suspicion of Southern customs. The Southern planter was pictured as being aristocratic and un-American, more like the English landed gentry than what had become (to Northerners) the American ideal. Visitors from the North also decried the inefficiency of the system. Frederick Law Olmsted, a writer interested in agriculture, visited the South and published a book, *The Cotton Kingdom*, in which he compared the efficiency of slave laborers with free Northern laborers. According to Olmsted, it took slaves four times as long to do a menial job as it did paid Northern laborers, and four house slaves did a sloppier job than one paid servant or housewife in the North. With prime hands costing about $2,000 plus food, clothing and shelter, he came to the conclusion that paid workers would save money and reduce the cost of cotton.

While many European immigrants who worked in Northern mills lived in dire poverty, Northern propagandists kept the public stirred up over conditions found on some plantations in the South. Harriet Beecher Stowe's *Uncle Tom's Cabin*—a maudlin novel about black Topsy and white Little Eva and the wicked overseer who beat slaves into submission—became a bestseller. It was imitated by many an aspiring novelist who had never been south but had read abolitionist propaganda.

Many churches in the North—particularly Presbyterians, Baptists, and Methodists—made a religious crusade of the effort to abolish slavery and so enraged their Southern congregations that the Southerners split off and formed their own denominations.

By 1860, many Northerners pictured Southerners as lazy, luxury-loving idlers who drank juleps on the verandas of huge mansions and watched sadistic overseers beat their helpless slaves. In some cases this may have been a true picture. There are bad apples in most barrels. But the fact that it was even possible gave Abolitionist missionaries fuel for their fiery crusade.

In the South, many thinking people felt that slavery was inefficient and perhaps even morally wrong. As early as 1775, Henry Laurens told his son, "I abhor slavery." Laurens and other thoughtful South Carolinians had urged the gradual emancipation of slaves by law, but now that cotton ruled, the idea was opposed by most of the population. The South had a tiger by the tail and could not let go.

14

The
Slaves' Life

By 1860 most thoughtful Southerners knew that slavery was wrong and could not continue in a democracy. Although a high tariff on foreign manufactured goods and unfair freight rates were more important issues, abolition had been seized upon in the North as a propaganda ploy. All the differences between an industrial culture and an agricultural culture were condensed and blamed upon slavery. Agitators, both Northern and Southern, had convinced the American public that slavery was what the fight was all about.

As "the peculiar institution" was decried by the Northern press, Southerners rallied stubbornly to defend their way of life, proclaiming that Southern planters were different from any other slave owners. Their slaves lived and prospered, they said, while those of the Indies died. The original Fundamental Constitutions for South Carolina had inaugurated a feudal society in the colony, and blacks were bound to their masters as feudal serfs had been bound to the soil. They were well-fed, housed and cared for. Slavery had been an institution even in Biblical times, the argument continued, and there was no use trying to change it.

More to the point (although not used as a justification), the production of rice and cotton depended upon a servile work force able to stand hard labor in hot, humid weather, and the importation of black Africans seemed the ideal answer. The fact that these people had no choice in the matter and no way of bettering their situation was overlooked for the sake of expediency.

In reality, the life of black slaves in the South was neither the hell on earth described by Northern propagandists nor the sylvan idyll painted by Southerners.

During the early colonial years, most slaves had been brought over from Africa. Many had been kidnapped from their homelands by black slavers, herded to the African coast, and crammed into ships captained, mainly, by New Englanders. The sanitary conditions were dreadful, and many died before reaching America.

Although a few of these Africans were of the warrior caste— Ashantis, Mandingos and others—these nomadic hunters and warriors were hard to catch. Most of the slaves had been farmers and were used to hard, continuous labor in their own towns and villages in West Africa—members of the Ibo, Ewe, Bifada, Bakongo, Wolof, Bambars, Ibibio, Serer and Arada tribes. They had lived in organized, isolated communities, with definite moral and ethical codes and a religion much like that of the Indians, believing in a Supreme Being and many minor gods. In Africa, warrior tribes had always preyed on peaceful tribes, using their captives as workers or selling them to other tribes. It was these warriors who kidnapped their neighbors for sale to white traders on the seacoast.

The shock of capture and transport was made worse by the fact that most of these people could not understand any African dialect but their own, and they certainly knew no English. One captured African, Gustavus Vassa, who later wrote his memoirs, tells of his terror on seeing white men, for fear they would eat him. Those slaves who were able to learn a few words of pidgin English could obey commands; the others were whipped into obedience.

When slaves arrived in Charleston, they were taken to a market and sold at auction. They were then marched, or taken in carts, to the plantations of their new masters, where they were given clothing and assigned living space. Hopefully there would be other slaves who understood their dialect and could teach them the routine of plantation life. Soon they would learn an Afro-English patois called "Gullah," which is thought to have been derived from an Angolan dialect.

Life in the "quarters" on a plantation became a mixture of African and English customs. Good masters, knowing that contented slaves made better workers, encouraged family life. Although slaves were not allowed to make legal contracts, they were often married by African tribal custom or, if the master were religious, by Christian clergymen. A pregnant slave worked in the fields until almost time for her delivery, but was usually allowed up to a month off after her baby was born. When she went back to work, the baby was brought to the fields and, with other children, was cared for by slave women who were too old to work, so that the mother could keep the baby nearby and suckle it on schedule.

Since most West Africans were polygamous, with one man keeping several wives in separate huts, the black women were used to being heads of their households, caring for the house and feeding and teaching the children for an absent father. On most Carolina plantations, cabins were assigned to mothers and children, except for some bachelor cabins. Fathers were welcomed home if they came. Often they brought crabs or fish or game caught in their time off.

Most plantation owners worked their slaves from sunup to sundown, with a rest period in the heat of the day. In their spare time, slaves were allowed to plant gardens behind their cabins, where they

A street of slave cabins at Boone Hall Plantation. Photograph courtesy of Bill R. Scroggins.

could grow greens and okra (an African import) and other vegetables and fruit to supplement their diet.

Basic supplies were rationed out by the planter's representative. The prescribed slave ration on most plantations was a weekly peck of corn (to be ground in a stone hand mill) and periodic rations of three pounds of salt pork, salt and molasses, with fresh beef and vegetables in season. Clothing was issued twice a year, at Easter and Christmas, and a new blanket every three years. The Easter issue was a rough cotton shirt and trousers for men and boys, a cotton shift dress for women and girls. Straw hats were often woven by the slaves if not provided by their masters. At Christmas, the ration included wool or cotton-and-wool clothing, and a pair of shoes. Food and clothing were taken for granted as a right, not as a reward for work.

The cabins in which the slaves lived varied from one plantation to the next, depending on the wealth or disposition of masters. Most were small, two-room wooden buildings with dirt floors and rough fireplaces. The slaves were expected to keep their cabins clean and sanitary, and some were required to whitewash them periodically.

Religious planters (most Low-Country landowners were either Church of England or Presbyterian) provided space for their slaves in their plantation churches. In the early days, services were also held in the quarters by black preachers. By the early 1800s, however, slave owners prohibited all-black religious meetings, fearing that preachers would stir up rebellion. Thereafter, slaves held services in secret and attended white churches with their masters as well.

Religion became a source of comfort for slaves in America. With a memory of tribal celebrations, they substituted the God of the white man for their all-powerful deity, the prophets and apostles for their minor gods. Jesus became the gentle comforter in tribulation, and heaven became a refuge after a life of toil. Spirituals, sung and danced during religious meetings, combined African rhythms with Christian lyrics. Presbyterian and Episcopalian ministers had little to offer the slaves, especially when they preached of hard work and obedience. Heaven, to these people, was escape from toil, and their clandestine religious services were a temporary respite from bondage.

Plantation life varied with the personalities of masters, overseers and slaves. There were good masters and bad, cruelty and kindness.

This surviving portion of Middleton Place House was originally built as a gentleman's guest wing, where during the Revolutionary period many patriots stayed. It now houses an important collection of furniture, paintings, silver, china, books and historic documents. Photograph courtesy of Middleton Place.

Henry Middleton, who started one of the first slave Sunday schools and tried conscientiously to care for the moral and physical well-being of his people, had over 2,000 blacks on his several plantations. Planters and their wives often thought of their slaves, both house servants and field hands, as their extended families. Natalie Sumter, daughter-in-law of the Gamecock, always called her slaves "my other children" in her diary, and spent at least part of every day caring for the sick and encouraging the downcast. In fact, it was taken for granted that planters' wives should care for sick servants. With the help of a home remedy book and their own common sense, these women ministered to both house servants and field hands unless there was serious illness; then the family physician was called from the nearest town. Southern ladies were famous for beauty and grace, but they were also the unsung heroines in times of illness or tragedy.

Not all plantation owners, however, were willing or able to spend such time and effort. The success of the crop depended on the work

of the slaves, and many planters left the supervision to hired
overseers, often paying them according to the amount of rice, indigo
or cotton produced. If the slaves produced less than the overseer
expected, he used a whip to spur them on. To help him keep the
slaves in line, he had black slave "drivers," who were in charge of
work gangs and had whips of their own. If slaves were willing to
work, if the weather permitted a good crop, and if the master,
overseer and drivers were reasonable, life could be bearable. But
short of running away, a slave had no choice except to take whatever
came his way. His only method of protest was indirect: He could
steal food, break tools, pretend to be ill or neglect his duties to slow
down the plantation process. The richest plantations were usually
those with the most contented slaves.

But all slaves did not live on large plantations. In fact, a majority
of slaveholders had fewer than ten slaves. Figures changed over the
years and in different parts of the state, but in St. George's Parish
in 1726, eighty percent of all households had slaves, and sixty percent
of slaveholders had ten slaves or less. At that time, however, twenty
percent of all slaves in the parish were owned by three people.

Tradesmen, professional men, merchants and craftsmen also
owned slaves. A doctor might have a slave to care for his office, as
well as a cook, a maid, a yardman and a nurse for his children. A
shopkeeper might have a slave to drive his delivery wagon, move his
stock, and even help clerk in his store. Craftsmen and mechanics,
many of them free blacks themselves, had slaves as helpers. In the
entire south by 1830, there were 3,775 free black slaveholders, over
half of them in Charleston and New Orleans.

In the cities, slaves had a better chance for education than on
plantations, where a slave child's education often consisted of
learning the Church of England Catechism, his duties to his master,
and the stories his mother told him. The Society for the Propagation
of the Gospel sent missionaries to Charleston in 1702 to educate all
Carolinians, and they started schools and Sunday schools for slaves
which were carried on for years. The Charleston Negro School,
begun by Alexander Garden in 1743, recognized the potential in
educating blacks and taught many to read and write before it closed
in 1765. White church organizations in Charleston also worked
among slaves and free blacks, teaching them when they showed
promise.

Zion School for children, Charleston.

In 1822, however, Denmark Vesey, a black minister, was discovered to be plotting to organize slaves to kill their masters. Vesey was executed and laws were made to keep slaves from learning to read subversive literature. The teaching of slaves was outlawed, and the education of free blacks was restricted, but the law was often ignored. At least fifteen schools were operated in Charleston by free blacks without interference by the authorities. Even on the plantations, masters often taught promising slaves to read and keep records, and white children often taught their black playmates. If a black man really wanted to learn to read and write, there were ways and means to learn. Like everything else, a slave's education depended on his circumstances and the character of those around him.

By the middle of the 1800s, slaves had become more and more necessary to their owners, and more expensive to purchase and keep. A South Carolinian with only ten slaves had an investment of $15,000 to $20,000 to protect. Liberating these slaves could mean a huge financial loss, even bankruptcy and ruin, to a majority of South Carolinians. They were not going to allow the Abolitionists to rob them!

15

The
War of Words

South Carolinians, more than any other Southerners, were ready to back out of the Union and fight for their way of life. A look at happenings on a national scale should help to bring the Carolina picture into focus.

John C. Calhoun had championed a reduced tariff and states' rights from the time he and Jackson tangled over Nullification. As he grew older and wiser, Calhoun tried harder to bring the whole country to his way of thinking. Believing in the importance of South Carolina to the nation, he felt that Northerners would give in before allowing a split. But events in the world outside of Carolina conspired to defeat his hopes.

In 1846, Zachary Taylor and Winfield Scott led American armies to defeat General Santa Anna in Mexico. The acquisition of Texas, California and lands in between followed, and the question of what would become of this territory was very important to both North and South. During the Mexican War, in 1846, Congressman David Wilmot, an anti-slavery Representative from Pennsylvania, attached a proviso to a bill to purchase territory that might be acquired from Mexico. Northern congressmen voted "for" and Southern congressmen "against," but there were enough moderates on both sides who wanted to keep the country together; they managed to defeat the measure.

By 1848 Texas had been admitted as a slave state and the Oregon Territory was non-slave. All the land from California east to Texas was undecided. In 1848 Zachary Taylor, hero of the Mexican War and a slaveowner, was elected President. By this time his Whig party was endorsed by both cotton growers and New England cotton manufacturers (whom the Democrats called "Lords of Lash and Lords of Loom").

Webster, Clay and Calhoun were still in the Senate, but all were now old men. With feeling running high, Henry Clay, famous as a compromiser, tried to find a solution to the question of the status of the new lands that would keep the peace. He proposed that California be admitted as a free state; that the rest of the territories acquired from Mexico be allowed to determine their own status; that New Mexico Territory be given some disputed land on the Mexican border; that slave trade be ended in the District of Columbia; and that a stricter fugitive slave law be passed. There was something in the proposal for each side.

John C. Calhoun, sixty-eight years old and so ill that he was unable to read his address to the Senate, opposed Clay's compromise. His speech, read by James Mason of Virginia, declared that the South had yielded ground on Missouri and Oregon and was now asked to yield on Mexican lands. Unless the South had equal rights in the territories, tighter fugitive slave laws, and an amendment to the Constitution to balance slave and free states, the nation would split apart. This was the hour when the South must take its stand.

A few days later Daniel Webster, also sixty-eight, made what seemed a conciliatory answer: If it came to a choice between abolition and the Union, the Union should be preserved. The North must return runaway slaves, since they were property under the constitution. California and New Mexico would probably vote against slavery on their own volition, and the whole country should agree to support the constitution.

Northern radicals, under the leadership of William H. Seward of New York, were enraged. Seward refused to believe that the Constitution should defend slavery and declared that a higher law than the Constitution was the law of God. President Taylor, like Jackson before him, now forsook his Southern heritage and joined Seward's fight. Calhoun was rumored to be organizing a Southern confederacy. President Taylor, again like Jackson, warned that he would hang any rebels who attempted to disrupt the Union.

Then both Taylor and Calhoun died, Calhoun gasping as he died,

"The South, the poor South! God knows what will become of her!" The new president, Millard Fillmore, favored Clay's ideas. Clay was by now suffering from exhaustion, but Stephen A. Douglas, the "Little Giant" from Illinois, pushed the compromise through. For a few more years the Union would remain.

It was Douglas, however, who opened the slavery question four years later. Hoping for Southern support in getting land for a transcontinental railroad, he introduced a bill to repeal the Missouri Compromise and allow Kansas and Nebraska to decide whether or not to have slaves, a principle known as "popular sovereignty." When the bill was passed in 1854, the fat was in the fire again. Abolitionist-backed settlers hurried to Kansas to vote against slavery, and hundreds of Southerners followed, armed and ready to assure a pro-slavery election. Two governments emerged, one pro- and one anti-slavery.

In 1856 John Brown, a mentally unbalanced anti-slavery anarchist, led his four sons and three other men in a raid on a pro-slavery settlement in Kansas, killing five people in cold blood. Anti-slavery agitators from Missouri crossed the boundary to clash with pro-slavery forces, turning Kansas into a bloody battlefield.

By 1858 Stephen A. Douglas, a Democrat, was running for senator in Illinois against Abraham Lincoln, candidate for the new Republican Party. Lincoln declared, "The government cannot endure permanently half slave, half free." The debates in their senatorial race brought the question of self-determination for the territories before the whole country. Lincoln lost that election, but he had gained the national limelight.

In 1859 John Brown, the Kansas anarchist, struck again, this time in Virginia. Hoping to arm slaves for insurrection, he and eighteen followers—five of them black—attempted to seize the federal arsenal at Harper's Ferry. When Brown was captured and hanged for treason, he became a martyr to the abolitionist cause. "John Brown's body lies a molderin' in the grave/His soul goes marching on!"—sung to the tune that later would become "The Battle Hymn of the Republic"—was popular throughout the North, much as the song "Blowin' in the Wind" became a harbinger of the Civil Rights movement of the 1960s.

With a presidential election coming the next year, the question of a Democratic candidate added fuel to the fire. The national convention, held in Charleston in April 1860, broke up before any decision was made, while in the North, Abraham Lincoln was nominated by the Republicans.

The fact that the Democratic convention was held in Charleston at all was a tribute to a group of Carolinians who had worked diligently to keep the party together, in hopes of influencing Northern Democrats to moderate their radical views ("Boll Weevils" of the 1860s). Hotheaded Carolinians had been talking Secession since before Calhoun stood Jackson down on Nullification, but there were many peace-loving souls who believed the Union could be preserved.

James L. Petigru, an early critic of the cotton economy and its dependence on slavery, had fought for many years to promote peaceful change. Joel Poinsett, Benjamin Perry, Waddy Thompson and William Grayson all cautioned against hasty action. After the fights over the Wilmot Proviso and the Clay Compromise, South Carolinians were split into Unionist and Secessionist camps.

John C. Calhoun had stood against compromise and, by his oratory and statesmanship, had been able to sway Congress. But there was no one of Calhoun's calibre to take his place. Robert Barnwell Rhett, who took his Senate seat, was a fire-eating Secessionist who lacked Calhoun's ability to persuade.

As early as June 1850, a convention of Southern states had been held in Tennessee; those in attendance were so badly divided that they adjourned and, when reconvened, backed away from Secession, with only South Carolina favoring such a drastic move. The next year, still hoping for support from other Southern states, the South Carolina Legislature began to prepare for war. A call was sent to other Southern states to meet in Montgomery in January 1852. Taxes were increased fifty percent to pay for equipment, and churches held services in favor of slavery. But when other states were reluctant to join the war effort, the public began to cool down. The Montgomery convention never met.

In this time of national controversy, South Carolinians argued among themselves as always. The moderates supported James L. Orr of Anderson, who became the leader of a group that favored keeping the Carolina Democratic Party within the national party in order to help shape party policy. They also believed in promoting industry and factories, creating opportunities for the poor and providing for public education. Rhett and his followers said such a program would undo the work of a whole generation.

When John Brown attacked Harper's Ferry, no one stopped to think that Brown was mentally deranged and the incident of little real significance. Instead, propagandists and preachers on both sides of the Mason-Dixon made the incident a subject for tirades. The whole country began to smoke and sputter again.

Since the two parts of the Democratic Party nominated two different candidates, it seemed sure that the Republican candidate, Abraham Lincoln, would win the election. And if he did, it would be only a matter of time before the South seceded.

As soon as the news of Lincoln's election was received, South Carolina called a state convention. Without waiting for the rest of the South, Carolinians voted unanimously to secede from the Union.

The Shooting War

The shooting war started when Fort Sumter was fired upon on April 12, 1861.

Major Robert Anderson of the United States Army moved his garrison from Fort Moultrie, the Revolutionary War fort on Sullivan's Island where Sergeant Jasper had saved the flag, to Fort Sumter, an unfinished pentagon-shaped stronghold built by the United States Government in the middle of Charleston Harbor, on the shoal where the British ships had gone aground in 1776. Fort Sumter had already taken thirty years to build, with underground fortifications that were considered impregnable to bombardment and five-foot-thick stone walls towering fifty feet above the water. Surrounded by water, it could be defended more easily than Fort Moultrie or Fort Johnson, on either side of the harbor entrance, even in its unfinished state.

The Secession of South Carolina was followed by like action in Mississippi, Florida, Alabama, Georgia, Louisiana and Texas. President Millard Fillmore, who would remain in office until March 4, hoped to avoid an explosion until Lincoln could take control.

Major Anderson and his eighty-five men (in a fort meant to be garrisoned by 650) were stuck out in the harbor without supplies. Rather than send armed assistance, the army sent an unarmed supply ship, *Star of the West*, in January, but it had to turn around when Citadel cadets manning a harbor battery opened fire.

Meanwhile, the South Carolina militia was strengthening Fort

Fort Sumter before attack, 1861. Photograph courtesy of the National Park Service, Department of the Interior.

Moultrie and training the hundreds of recruits who flocked in to keep the Yankees out of the South. Daily purchases of food from Charleston were allowed to the men of Fort Sumter, to keep Federal troops from coming to their aid before South Carolina was ready. Finally word reached Charleston that the newly inaugurated president, Abraham Lincoln, was sending a fleet to relieve Fort Sumter, by force if necessary. General Beauregard, the area commander of Confederate forces, sent a message to Major Anderson demanding immediate surrender. When Anderson asked for three days, he was warned that bombardment would begin in an hour.

Mary Boykin Chesnut, whose diary provides descriptions of many events during the war, described her vigil from the roof of the Mills House in Charleston. Her husband, former U.S. Senator James Chesnut, was an aide-de-camp to General Beauregard and in charge of harbor defense; he was somewhere out in the harbor area commanding Confederate artillery batteries. As the batteries from Fort Moultrie and Fort Johnson opened fire, she could see the shells bursting. Even at that fearful hour, her sense of humor triumphed. She writes of the other women on the hotel roof, "These women have all a satisfying faith. 'God is on our side,' they cry. When—I ask 'Why' Answer: 'Of course, He hates Yankees! You'll think that well of him.'"

Thirty-four hours and 3,000 shells later, Major Anderson surrendered. He was permitted a 100-gun salute to the American flag as it was lowered, then his Federal troops boarded the steamship *Isabel* for the North.

The war had begun. Four more states—North Carolina, Virginia, Tennessee and Arkansas—joined the Confederacy; Maryland, Kentucky and West Virginia remained neutral, to be known as "border states."

Now that the die was cast, both North and South plunged into the job of raising armies to blow each other to bits. It is hard to understand, now, how the South could have been so confident of victory. It is true that the high-ranking officers of the Confederacy, many of them West Pointers who had left the U.S. Army to fight for their states, were superior, in many cases, to their Northern counterparts. And Southern men were fighting for their homeland, which is always an incentive to fight with all one's might. Few Northern soldiers, except those who had been influenced by Abolitionist propaganda, were anxious to shoot their Southern counterparts, any more than poor Southern whites were anxious to fight for slavery. But with bugles blowing, flags waving and sabres flashing in the sunlight, men on both sides were panting for the glory of battle. Women cheered them as knights in armor, and preachers on both sides prayed for victory, sure that God was on the right side—their side.

The truth was that the Southern states had only a few factories and depended on agricultural staples—cotton, rice, tobacco and sugar cane—for most of their income, importing much of their food and almost all of their manufactured goods. Hoping that the mills in England and France would be so dependent on Southern cotton that they would help the Confederacy, the South continued to plant cotton as her main crop.

For the first three years of the war, mainland South Carolina saw almost nothing of Union troops. Union ships patrolled the coast, however, and in the fall of 1861, six months after Fort Sumter, rumor told of a big Union fleet being prepared to sail south.

A few owners of plantations on the sea islands, like William Elliott of Beaufort, advised the removal of slaves from the Port Royal-Hilton Head area, but most Carolinians thought the Union forces would attack Charleston. When the fleet arrived off Beaufort and began its bombardment, most plantation owners had time only to flee with a few belongings, leaving their homes and their slaves. Many burned their cotton fields to keep the Yankees from harvesting the crop.

South Carolina's sea island plantations grew the finest cotton in the world. The Federal government planned to take over the islands, remove slaves from the plantations and then pay them to grow cotton on land which would be confiscated and divided into forty-acre lots, then mortgaged to the blacks and paid for in cotton. To administer this program, missionaries would be settled with the blacks, to teach them to read and write and farm. While the army and navy were interested in turning cotton into money, the abolitionists were interested in teaching "contrabands," as freed slaves were called, how to take care of themselves.

The next four years in this area were a preview of the problems of Reconstruction, with well-meaning but inept Northern missionaries who were known as Gideon's Band, or Gideonites (Methodists from New York, Quakers from Philadelphia and Unitarians from Boston), in charge. They all had different plans for helping the blacks, and none of them knew anything about cotton farming. The Gullah language of the islanders created another difficulty.

By the end of the war, some of the black farmers had made a success of their farms, though most of them grew vegetables, refusing to grow cotton. Many of the black vegetable farmers of the sea islands today are descended from those "contrabands."

The Union Army took over the town of Beaufort, pillaging the planters' homes and using some for quarters. Gardens were trampled and furniture smashed. Hilton Head became a fortified refueling port, and Port Royal Sound became a deep anchorage for Union ships.

Charleston was a different matter. The struggle to keep South Carolina's chief port open to Confederate ships was one of the most important of the war. Blockade runners were the lifeblood of the Confederacy, bringing supplies from England and the Continent, and Charleston was one of the few ports to remain open throughout the war, until Sherman's Army forced its evacuation.

Confederate batteries were placed on the islands along the coast, for the defense of Charleston. When federal ships landed raiding parties along the coast, the fighting was intense.

The first real effort to take Charleston came in June 1862, when Federal troops under General Hunter, from occupied Beaufort, landed on James Island but were unable to take the fort at Secessionville. In April 1863, an attempt by the Federal ship *Ironsides* and eight monitors to break through the harbor defenses and bombard the city was repulsed with heavy loss. In the summer of 1863, after many land and sea attacks by Federal forces, Battery Wagner, on Morris Island, finally surrendered, giving the Yankees a foothold within five miles of Charleston. Here, on piles in the swamp, they mounted batteries of artillery—including the deadly eight-inch Parrot gun known as the "Swamp Angel"—that wreaked havoc in lower Charleston for months on end. But Charleston refused to surrender. Contemporary accounts tell of people learning to live with shells falling around them, and even joking about Yankee gunners.

The Southerners had style, they loved a good scrap, and they were so sure they could lick any number of Yankees that, for a while, they had the Yankees convinced of it too. Early in the war, when Generals Beauregard, Johnston, Wade Hampton and "Stonewall" Jackson turned McClellan's army back toward Washington at the first battle of Manassas (or Bull Run), the V.I.P.'s from Washington, who had to flee before they were trampled by the retreating Federal troops, were also convinced.

The Union plan for the war was to capture Richmond, blockade the Southern ports, and control the Mississippi and Tennessee rivers. Using two armies, one in the east and one in the west, they would crush the Confederate forces in between. The Confederate plan was to capture Washington, go through Maryland and Pennsylvania, and cut the North in two. But while the Confederates were winning against the Union Army of the East, the Union Army of the West was winning in Kentucky and Tennessee. By the summer of 1862, New Orleans had fallen and Vicksburg, Mississippi was under siege by combined army and navy forces of the Union.

In the East, Union General McClellan, who had been sitting outside Washington with his Army of the Potomac, started for Richmond in March 1862, by way of Yorktown. Stonewall Jackson then threatened Washington, forcing McClellan to detach part of his army. General Joe Johnston kept McClellan out of Richmond but was badly wounded and passed his command on to Robert E. Lee.

Union General John Pope was now ordered to replace the unpopular McClellan but, with 75,000 men to Lee's 48,000 Confederates, was defeated at the Second Battle of Manassas (Bull Run). So McClellan was put back in command and met Lee's army at Antietam Creek in September 1862. Although Antietam was not a clear-cut defeat for the South, since Lee's army retreated in good order, the Confederate drive was ended there. News of the battle convinced Britain and France that the Confederacy might not win, and thereafter all British and French military and financial aid was cut off.

The South was not licked yet, however, although armaments and supplies were getting scarce and troop replacements were slow. General J.E.B. Stuart made a cavalry raid into Pennsylvania in October, and in December Lee slaughtered a Union Army under General Burnsides at Fredericksburg. In January 1863, Lee and Jackson drove off a Union army under General Joseph Hooker at Chancellorsville, but Jackson was killed.

Then came Gettysburg—where Lee, Longstreet, Ewell, Hill and Pickett fought the most famous battle of the war against General George G. Meade and his Army of the Potomac. After dreadful casualties inflicted by both armies, Lee was forced to retreat into Virginia. On that same day, Vicksburg fell to Grant's Union Army in the West, cutting off Arkansas, Louisiana and Texas by giving the Federals control of the Mississippi River.

Grant was now ordered back to Tennessee to take command of the Armies of the West. He was joined by General Sherman and his Army of the Tennessee (Union armies were named for rivers, Confederate armies for towns or landmarks) at Lookout Mountain, near Chattanooga. Together they overwhelmed General Braxton Bragg's Confederate Army, leaving the way open to Atlanta and all points south and east. Grant was ordered east then, leaving Sherman to move into the fertile farmlands of Georgia and the Carolinas.

General William Tecumseh Sherman, even 100 years after his death, is still considered a fiend incarnate by many Southerners—the epitome of Yankeeism. His campaign through the three states has been compared to the vandalism of Attila the Hun, crippling the economy of South Carolina long afterwards.

Sherman himself felt that his scorched-earth policy would save lives in the long run. By cutting off supplies to the men fighting an already losing battle, he would shorten the war. He gave orders that

General William Tecumseh Sherman. Photograph courtesy of South Caroliniana Library, University of South Carolina.

his men should burn only supplies and not homes—but then, like Pontius Pilate, washed his hands of the consequences of his campaign.

Unlike many of the abolitionist-inspired Union generals, Sherman was not fighting against slavery or even against the wealthy Southern aristocracy which so infuriated middle-class Northerners. In his bachelor days, after graduating from West Point, he had been stationed at the Augusta Arsenal and at Fort Moultrie, and had made many good friends in both cities. At the time Carolina seceded,

Sherman, aged forty-four, was serving as superintendent of the Louisiana Military Academy. Although he loved the South, he felt that the breakup of the United States was treason and must be stopped, and he blamed the hotheads of South Carolina for making the break.

When Louisiana seceded, Sherman parted from his cadets with tears in his eyes. When war was declared, he was commissioned as a colonel and fought at Manasses, where he was one of the last Union officers to retreat. Given command of a division in Tennessee, he supported Grant at Shiloh, and when Grant was ordered east to fight against Lee's army, Sherman was left to reorganize the Army of the Tennessee for an attack on Atlanta and a campaign through the South.

Because he knew and respected the courage of Southerners, Sherman knew that fear of death would not keep Southern men from fighting; but fear for their wives and children could demoralize the Confederate Army. More important, his plan would cut off supplies from Lee's army in Virginia. Atlanta was a rail center, Augusta the site of a major Confederate powder works, and Charleston and Savannah were still open for blockade runners to carry cotton to England and bring in munitions. Most important, all through the fertile midsections of Georgia and the Carolinas were farms loaded with food and livestock. The best way to stop the supplies was to kill or steal the stock, burn barns and ruin fields.

Sherman's men were not the drafted shopkeepers and factory workers of the army in the East. Midwestern frontiersmen, poor whites and small farmers, they were tough and wiry and often mean. There were some older men, but thousands of them were under the age of eighteen. Sherman called them "my little devils." Battle gear was stripped down to a blanket and poncho, a tin cup, cartridge box and rifle (the new sixteen-shot repeater). When there was no supply wagon, troops were supposed to forage for themselves. Discipline was reduced to a minimum.

It was this crowd of unruly young hoodlums, 62,000 strong, who captured Atlanta and were told to burn only public buildings but to save private homes. In fact, "they were potentially cruel and heartless pillagers, many of whom awaited only the opportunity to plunder, burn and rape." At first only railroad shops, depots, factories and warehouses were burned, according to orders, but then the soldiers began looting stores and finding liquor and valuables. Even the sentries joined in. Soon fires were burning all over town, and by dawn on November 15, 1864, 200 acres of Atlanta lay in ashes.

After Sherman left Atlanta, telegraph lines were cut in all directions along the line of march. Though prepared to mow down any Confederate resistance, Sherman hoped to avoid battles if no one knew where his army was. Splitting his forces in two, with a minimum of supply wagons to slow him down, he marched the armies across Georgia on parallel courses about eighty miles apart. They burned towns and farms, stopped to sack the state capital at Milledgeville, and ended up in Savannah six weeks later to give the city to President Lincoln as a Christmas present. Sherman's telegram from Savannah was the first word the War Department had received of his whereabouts since his departure from Atlanta.

Savannah was not sacked. General William Hardee, in command of its defenses, had only 9,000 troops—most of them old men, boys and soldiers pushed eastward by Sherman's march. Under orders from General Beauregard, Hardee evacuated his army by night over a bridge built secretly—in four days, under the very nose of Sherman—across the Savannah River. Hardee's troops were needed to fight in South Carolina. Sherman's army moved into Savannah, which was saved to become a Union supply port, in time for Christmas.

From Washington, Grant urged Sherman to move his army immediately by sea to aid in defeating Lee in Virginia. Since this was not a direct order, Sherman decided to march on through the Carolinas.

Ever since Atlanta, Sherman's army had been burdened with what now amounted to thousands of freed slaves who had flocked from the devastated plantations along the march. Arranging for them to be transported to the sea islands of the Beaufort area, Sherman ordered land to be confiscated for taxes from absent plantation owners and parcelled out in forty-acre lots to the "contrabands." Then he started his army northward, across the Savannah and into South Carolina. General Howard's column moved north from Beaufort, while General Slocum's column moved along the Savannah River, then north to meet the other forces in Columbia. Kilpatrick's cavalry skirmished between, to intercept any Confederate attacks.

South Carolina would be punished for starting the war. Sherman is quoted as saying, "I'm going to march to Richmond . . . and when

I go through South Carolina it will be one of the most horrible things in the history of the world."

Even with Sherman's Georgia campaign as a warning, South Carolinians could make no real preparation to stop him. Hardee and Stevenson, both short-handed, were ordered to hold the line as long as possible and then fall back to defend Charleston. If Charleston fell, then they were to retreat to Columbia. Though hard-pressed in Virginia, Lee sent General Wade Hampton home, with a cavalry division under General Matthew Butler, to defend South Carolina against Sherman's 60,000 well-supplied and seasoned troops.

General Joe Wheeler, sent with his cavalry to harry Sherman's flanks and hoping to protect homes in Sherman's path, sent a note through the lines saying that he would promise not to burn any more cotton if Sherman would burn no houses. Sherman replied, "I hope you will burn all the cotton to save us the trouble. It has proven a curse to our country."

The first real resistance the Union Army met was at the Salkahatchie River, where General Hardee and 10,000 troops dug in to stop General Howard and the northern branch of the Union Army. In the boggy swampland, Hardee guarded the stream crossings with cannon. Sherman's men plunged into the swamp up to their necks and made their way across to flank the Confederates at Buford's Bridge. The outnumbered Confederates were forced to retreat, but Sherman's troops had suffered terrible mutilation by the blasts of cannon fire. This was the last major engagement in South Carolina. Except for skirmishes, the blue coats were able to tramp through the state almost unopposed.

At the Edisto and North rivers, the advance was halted by Confederate forces, but only until the Union forces could send a brigade around to flank the small Confederate groups. Everywhere, it was a matter of huge numbers of blue uniforms against handfuls of gray.

In Orangeburg the Yankees found several houses already on fire. A merchant had set fire to the cotton in his own store, and the fire had spread. As the town burned, Sherman visited an Orangeburg orphanage and posted guards to protect the children, leaving provisions for them.

Kilpatrick and his cavalry were sent by Sherman to destroy Barnwell. As the town burned, the general and his officers staged a ball in the hotel, where they danced and sang with the freed black women.

As soon as Sherman was out of the swampy Low Country, he made for Columbia, ignoring Charleston and the confederate troop build-up waiting to defend the port. He sent Kilpatrick's cavalry off toward Augusta to keep the Confederate troops there busy while his army took lightly-defended Columbia. Coming out of Augusta, General Joseph Wheeler met Kilpatrick with 2,000 Confederate cavalry in Aiken; after a wild mounted battle in the streets, Wheeler sent Kilpatrick and his men off with several wagonloads of Union wounded. Wheeler was congratulated for saving Augusta, but Sherman's main army was already outside Columbia.

On February 15, 1865, Sherman's army camped overlooking the city. Columbia was jammed with refugees from Charleston who had thought Sherman would attack that important seaport and leave Columbia alone. With nine generals in Columbia—including Hampton, Beauregard and Chesnut—there was still no plan for the city's defense. General Wade Hampton, in command of all Confederate cavalry, refused to allow the mayor to destroy the liquor supply and surrender the city; until Federal shells began to fall and the host of 60,000 began to move in. Then Hampton and his men rode out through the northern suburbs while Beauregard and his staff left by another route.

The mayor, Dr. Thomas Goodwin, rode out on the morning of February 17 to ask that the citizens of the surrendered city be accorded the treatment prescribed in civilized warfare. The Mother Superior of the Ursuline Convent, who had taught Sherman's daughter in Ohio, asked protection for the convent.

At two P.M., Sherman and his staff rode in. An American flag was raised above the Statehouse. Earlier, the general had dictated orders that public buildings—including railroad depots, factories and machineshops—be burned, but libraries, hospitals and private dwellings were to be spared. What happened from then on has been argued for more than 100 years.

Sherman's memoirs and other Union soldiers' accounts describe long rows of cotton bales, burning in the streets, when they entered town; these were doused to put out the fire. Some said the cotton smoldered and began to burn again. All accounts attest to the presence of untold gallons of liquor, some brought by refugees to the city, some in the cellars of Columbians, and some in stores and warehouses.

At first it seemed that the army would obey orders and the city would be saved. When fire spread to shops and private homes, Federal officers set the troops to work fighting the fire, but with wind whipping the flames, the blaze was soon out of control—as were the troops. According to eyewitness accounts, Sherman's soldiers were undisciplined and running wild. Full of stolen liquor, they acted as pillaging armies have throughout history—only this time with the excuse that Carolinians were being punished for starting the war.

There were no official reports of white women being raped, though if it had occurred it would have been kept quiet in those Victorian days. Black women are known to have been victims. Historian William Gilmore Simms, who was in Columbia during the sack, wrote, "The poor Negroes were victimized by their assailants, many of them being left in a condition little short of death."

Churches were ransacked and the convent which Sherman had promised to protect was looted and burned by drunken soldiers, the

The ruins of Columbia, 1865, after Sherman and his army sacked the city. Photograph courtesy of the South Carolina Historical Society.

gold vessels from the altar stolen as schoolgirls were saying the Rosary in chapel.

The Reverend Peter J. Shand, Rector of Trinity Episcopal Church, was surrounded by soldiers and the communion silver stolen as he tried to carry it to safety. South Carolina College, which was being used as a hospital, was burned, killing many wounded soldiers.

It is true that many Union soldiers fought heroically to put out fires and protect frightened civilians from the drunken mob, but their compassion was so outweighed by the depravity of the majority that the people of Columbia would carry hatred of Blue Coats to their graves.

By midafternoon on February 18, a change of the wind finally stopped the spread of fire, and sober troops were ordered in to control the rioters. Almost three-quarters of the city had been destroyed—1,386 houses, stores and other buildings burned to the ground. By February 20, Sherman's Army had disappeared, leaving women and old men to care for their homeless families and begin the desperate task of rebuilding.

They were equal to the job. Southern ladies, delicate in the drawing room, showed their true strength and determination. Emma LeConte, the daughter of a chemistry professor at South Carolina College, remained on campus through most of the fire. She wrote in her diary, "The Yankee officers . . . paid tribute to the women of the State, saying they were the most firm, obstinate and ultra rebel set of women they had encountered."

Before he left, Sherman ordered half of his cattle herd and half of the rations in his wagons left for the use of the people in the city. Despite his sympathy for the destitute citizens, Sherman said, years later, of the sack of Columbia, "Though I never ordered it and never wished it, I have never shed many tears over the event, because I believe it hastened what we all fought for, the end of the war."

As he left Columbia and headed northward, Sherman was followed by thousands of freed slaves, escaped prisoners and prostitutes. The army's most famous camp follower was Marie Boozer, who was "under the protection" of General Kilpatrick and rode in a handsome black carriage stolen from the Elmore family. Daughter of a famous Columbia beauty of doubtful reputation, Marie left Columbia with Kilpatrick; she later left him to marry a millionaire and after that a French count.

The march toward the North Carolina border was like the rest of the campaign. Harried by Wheeler's cavalry but fighting no major battles, the two columns drove through the countryside, destroying crops and livestock, burning barns and occasional homes. Much of the town of Winnsboro was burned, but the Reverend Obear's boarding school for girls escaped with only broken windows. It was probably at Winnsboro that Sherman received word that Charleston and Wilmington had been surrendered and the Confederate Armies evacuated. General Joseph Johnston had now been ordered to halt Sherman's advance.

As the army swept into Camden, Confederate soldiers, captured in a skirmish in defense of the town, said, "It isn't fair. The Yankees have guns they load up on Sunday and shoot all the rest of the week." These sixteen-shot repeating rifles were one of the major reasons for the defeat of the Confederacy. While Confederate soldiers had to stop and reload after every shot, Union soldiers could keep going as they fired sixteen rounds.

In Camden two railroad depots were burned, along with a bridge, a flour mill, a warehouse and 2,000 bales of cotton. The town's stores were gutted by looters; furniture, food and silverware hidden by the citizens were discovered and taken. Also captured in the woods were the funds of both Camden banks, which had been loaded on wagons to escape the Yankees—$3,700 in gold and silver, and almost two million dollars in Confederate bonds.

On the way to Cheraw, the Union army was held up for four days at Lynch's Creek, which had flooded beyond its banks until it was almost a mile wide. Confederate cavalry attacked as the Union soldiers were trying to make pontoon bridges for a safe crossing. Finally the Union men were ordered to strip and wade or swim across, carrying clothing and rifles above their heads. As they came out on the opposite bank, they were attacked by Confederates and went into battle naked except for boots and hats.

Cheraw, on the Pee Dee River, was full of valuables shipped for safety from Charleston, including fine wine and brandy. In the saturnalia that followed the liberation of the liquor, a Confederate powder magazine was set afire, demolishing three houses and killing six soldiers and several civilians. The army then crossed the Pee Dee, leaving most of the town in flames.

As the army crossed the North Carolina border, one Union officer wrote in his journal, "South Carolina may have been the cause of the whole thing, but she has had an awful punishment."

On April 9, General Robert E. Lee surrendered the Army of Northern Virginia to General Grant at Appomattox Court House. Sherman continued his march through North Carolina. When the army reached Raleigh, General Joseph Johnston, realizing the end of the war was near, met with Sherman to negotiate an honorable surrender. Sherman had heard the terms of Lee's surrender and proposed very much the same terms.

The shooting war was over, but another dreadful struggle was to follow, when the hate-filled Northern politicians would try to break the still-strong spirit of the South.

17

Reconstruction

Abraham Lincoln's assassination by John Wilkes Booth, on April 14, 1865, was a greater tragedy for South Carolina than Sherman's march, though few Carolinians realized it at the time.

To Southerners, Lincoln was the evil being who had caused the war. Actually, as President, he had an almost religious conviction that slavery must be abolished and the aristocratic plantation system smashed. Led by Thaddeus Stevens of Pennsylvania, a group had tried to undermine Lincoln's conciliatory policy toward the Confederacy throughout the war.

Stevens was seventy-three years old, sick and crippled. His stubborn jaw, long thin nose and piercing eyes gave him the look of a zealot. Bald for years, he wore a coal-black wig that made his haggard features seem even more sinister. He lived with a pretty mulatto housekeeper and had many black friends. Stevens' plan for the South included not only the abolishment of slavery but also the confiscation of plantations and redistribution of lands to freed slaves. He had a bitter hatred for aristocrats and a personal anger at the Confederate Army for burning his iron foundry near Gettysburg. Intelligent, with sharp, sarcastic wit, Stevens was able to keep the Republican Party under his thumb even though he was often too weak to stand in the Senate to make speeches. He wanted Southerners to be beaten into submission and made to accept their former slaves as social equals.

When Andrew Johnson became President after Lincoln's death,

Stevens and the Radical Republicans tried their extreme ideas on him and were surprised to find that he was no pushover. Born in poverty in North Carolina and trained as a tailor's apprentice, Johnson had come up the hard way. When he started a tailor shop in Tennessee, he was so well liked that politicians crowded his shop for discussions. Soon he had climbed the political ladder to the U.S. Senate, and then to the vice presidency. Where few Radical Republicans knew slavery and the plantation system first-hand, Johnson had lived with both and knew Southerners well. With his poor white background, he hated aristocrats but, unlike the Radicals, he also hated and distrusted blacks, for he had competed with them in the labor market.

In May 1865, President Johnson issued a pardon for most Confederates, restoring to them all property—except slaves and some of the lands on the sea islands, which had been confiscated and redistributed by Sherman—if they would swear allegiance to the United States and obey the laws concerning the abolition of slavery which had been made during the war. The exceptions to this pardon were all generals and high Confederate officials, as well as those who now owned $20,000 or more. When ten percent of the voters of 1860 had sworn to uphold the results of the war, each state could meet and draw up a constitution, elect officials and be considered "reconstructed." Since Congress had gone home for the summer and would not reconvene until December, the President was able to make this move without organized opposition from the Radicals.

Benjamin F. Perry of Greenville had fought against Secession to the very end and then decided that "as the state was determined to go to hell, he would go along with her." Perry was appointed by Johnson as provisional governor until South Carolinians could qualify to elect a governor of their choice.

South Carolina was occupied by Federal troops, and at this early date they were generally commanded by qualified officers who kept them in line. The Freedmen's Bureau was financed by the Federal government but was led by Northern missionaries in the enormous job of rehabilitating thousands of freed slaves, who now roamed the state with no means of support except funds doled out by the government. In the early days, Bureau members were conscientiously dedicated to the education and moral uplifting of blacks. Schools were manned by teachers who were paid by the Freedmen's Bureau, and Northern churches sponsored the building and maintenance of black colleges, some of which are in operation still. But since this bureau had jurisdiction over all relationships between blacks and whites, as well as custody and redistribution powers over unused land, it was no time at all before it was taken over by self-seeking politicians.

Lincoln's idea for Reconstruction had been a constitutional rehabilitation of the Confederacy, treating states as though they were still members of the Union. Trying to carry on Lincoln's ideas, Johnson had proceeded with this plan. The Radical Republicans in Congress, however, felt that the Confederate States should be treated as a hostile foreign government and made to pay for the war.

When South Carolina and the other Southern states had elected legislators and governors, and ratified the Thirteenth Amendment (which abolished slavery) and had sworn allegiance to the United States, they expected to be treated as prodigals and welcomed in good standing. Congressmen and senators were elected to be sent to Washington. A new state constitution was passed, with blacks no longer considered property and with some moderate reforms in taxation. James L. Orr of Anderson, who had been a U.S. Congressman before the war and who had tried to keep South Carolina in the Union by cooperation with the National Democratic Party, was elected governor. If the other men elected to office had been anti-secessionists, there might have been a chance for a reasonable government. But South Carolina loved her heroes, and the people elected Confederate generals and pre-war statesmen to public office. When South Carolina's representatives to Congress arrived in Washington, the Radicals refused to allow them to be seated.

Back in Carolina, wandering, unemployed ex-slaves were becoming a problem, and a set of laws known as the Black Code was passed by the Legislature. These laws provided a harsher criminal code for blacks than for whites, denying blacks the right to testify against whites, allowing them to work only in agriculture and servile jobs and permitting moderate whipping as a punishment for apprentices. To South Carolina's former slave-owners, these laws seemed necessary to control vagrancy and end the labor shortage. To Northern Abolitionists, they seemed almost a return to slavery.

To end what they considered the persecution of blacks, radicals in Washington pushed through a civil rights law giving all men born

Slave children at the Reconstruction school on Sea Island. Photograph courtesy of Wofford College.

in the States equal protection under the law and the right to vote (if they had not been disenfranchised as Rebels or felons). The Freedmen's Bureau had absolute power to direct civil and political action against black citizens. The Fourteenth Amendment to the Constitution was then drafted, embodying these principles, and sent to all the states for ratification. When the Southern states refused to ratify it, they were regarded as treasonous and still in need of punishment.

As long as Andrew Johnson was President, he tried to keep the Washington Radicals in line by vetoing legislation that he thought would be disastrous for the South. Many of his vetoes were overridden, however. A plan for military occupation of the South was passed over his veto on March 2, 1867. This radical reconstruction plan divided the south into five military districts, each under the jurisdiction of an army general whose troops would enforce his orders.

To be relieved of martial law and again allowed representation in Congress, a state was required to have a constitution written by a convention for which delegates were elected by all the male citizens of the state, white and black. The state government created by this constitution would have to be acceptable to Congress and would have to ratify the Fourteenth Amendment.

At the same time, Congress passed laws limiting certain powers of the President, including his power over the army. All army orders must now be approved by General Ulysses S. Grant, General-in-Chief of the Army and a puppet of Congress. The radical steamroller was ready to flatten all opposition.

With Thaddeus Stevens ruling the House and Charles Sumner in power in the Senate, and with Samuel Chase as Chief Justice of the Supreme Court, South Carolina was doomed. Sumner, a radical abolitionist from Massachusetts, had ridiculed Senator Pierce Butler and his state, South Carolina, back in 1856, during a debate over slavery in Kansas. Butler's cousin, Preston Brooks, had then attacked Sumner with a cane in the Senate chamber. Sumner had been injured in both body and pride, and he hated all Carolinians. A sincere abolitionist, he was interested in the welfare of blacks, but he was more interested in making the South grovel for her sin of defiance.

What money was left in the South was ripe, now, for plucking. The next few years were jokingly known in the corrupt Congress as an "era of good stealing."

A military governor, General Daniel E. Sickles, replaced in August 1867 by General E.R.S. Canby, was sent to the District of North and South Carolina. On July 5, Congress forbade the vote to anyone who had held even the smallest civil or military office in the South. In South Carolina, twice as many blacks as whites were registered.

The Freedmen's Bureau, which had been taken over by crooked politicians, told the poor, illiterate black men that white Southerners would put them back in slavery if they did not vote Republican. The Union League, controlled by Northern radicals, organized all black voters and took them to the polls to vote for representatives to the constitutional convention. The Constitutional Convention of 1868 consisted of twenty-three white Carolinians, twenty-five white carpetbaggers, fifty-seven black Carolinians and nineteen black carpetbaggers.

It was at this time that the terms "scalawag" and "carpetbagger" came into Southern slang. A scalawag was a white Southerner who supported the Northern radicals to gain money and political power. A carpetbagger (named for the cheap suitcases made from pieces of old rugs) was a Northerner who came south to take political office in order to gain political power and line his pockets. Both scalawags and carpetbaggers were paid huge bribes by the Radical Republicans in Washington.

The Carpetbagger Constitution of 1868 was more liberal than any in the past and was disparaged by most white Carolinians. It abolished imprisonment for debt; eliminated property ownership as a requirement for election to public office; required public education, supported by the state, to be open to all races; allowed intermarriage of the races; and legalized divorce in cases of adultery. Children of both races were required to attend school, either public or private, until the age of sixteen. Although these laws seem reasonable today, the change was too abrupt for Southerners living over 100 years ago.

As soon as the constitution was written, a new government was formed with seventy-five percent of those elected being Republican. The new governor was Robert K. Scott, who had come south from Ohio with the Union Army. The government under Scott and his

Northern carpetbaggers derived their name from bags made of carpet which they carried.

successor, Franklin J. Moses, has been acknowledged by Northerners and Southerners alike to be one of the most drunken, licentious and corrupt assemblies of all time. When General Grant became President in 1869, there was nothing to hold back skulduggery and massive thievery in the Federal government. With the South prostrated under military rule, the Reconstruction governments happily voted taxes and land grabs to line their pockets. In South Carolina, landholders were taxed until they were unable to pay more, and then their lands were confiscated for taxes. Huge appropriations for printing and legislative supplies, as well as fraudulent bond issues, took millions of taxpayers' dollars; most of the money went into legislators' pockets. A saloon was maintained in the State House at taxpayers' expense, furnishing a gallon of whiskey and a dozen cigars a day for every member of the Legislature. Thousands of dollars appropriated for furnishing the State House were spent on furnishing the homes of legislators.

There were a few educated and conscientious assemblymen, both black and white, who tried to keep order in the squalid atmosphere of the State House. Among the blacks, Robert Smalls, a former slave, was a talented speaker who kept up a fight for better conditions for blacks. At the beginning of the war, when Federal forces had taken over the Port Royal area, Smalls had taken his absent master's ship, *The Planter*, and had gone over to the Union. With this ship and black militia from Hilton Head, he had raided along the coast, carrying slaves to freedom in Port Royal. Known as "The Gullah Statesman," Smalls was less corrupt than most members of the General Assembly. At one time he was convicted of taking a bribe (which was almost standard procedure during Reconstruction), but he was pardoned by Governor Wade Hampton and was so well-liked that he was sent to Congress from his largely black district for years after Reconstruction.

Robert Brown Elliott, a black from Massachusetts who was Speaker of the House during Reconstruction, claimed to have been educated at Eton and used his legal skill to fight for racial equality. T.L. Cardozo, a free-born black Carolinian whose father was Jewish, was secretary of state and then treasurer of the Reconstruction government. A graduate of Glasgow University and a London theology school, Cardozo was better educated than most carpetbaggers and scalawags in the Assembly, although his politics were said to be as corrupt as any.

Robert Smalls, a former slave who fought for improved conditions for blacks, was known as "The Gullah Statesman."

Most black members of the legislature, however, were unable to read or write and were manipulated by white politicians into approving their dishonest schemes for stealing South Carolina blind. Believing that they were being helped by the white men, these black legislators were really being set up to take the blame for the illegal acts of Yankee Reconstructionists when the latter scuttled the ship of state and headed north. But for eight long years—from 1868 until 1876—the people of South Carolina lived quietly under this corrupt government, with the threat of military intervention if they tried to protect their property.

Former Confederate officers and statesmen, unable to vote, put their energy into rebuilding their devastated lands, while women stayed at home. Many former slaves returned to work on the plantations after they found that freedom could mean starvation. Some simply worked for food and shelter until the land began to produce again. They were paid wages when cash was available, often having to wait until the crops were harvested. Slowly, in spite of the corruption in the State House, the people of South Carolina, white and black, began to climb up out of despair.

White South Carolinians, knowing that the Radicals were looking for excuses to punish them, were careful not to stir up any trouble. Bands of wandering former slaves stole to keep from starving. Black militia blamed white landowners for any clashes with the vagrants, and militiamen themselves were apt to rape, burn and steal. But there were surprisingly few whites convicted of racial wrongs.

It was at this time that the Ku Klux Klan made its appearance. Claude G. Bowers tells of its founding in Pulaski, Tennessee in 1865. Six penniless young men, former Confederate soldiers, decided on Christmas Eve to start a club, with initiations and high jinks to amuse themselves, their families and girls. They raided linen closets and went riding off on horseback in the middle of the night to call on their sweethearts.

The original ride had been for fun, but the organization soon changed when it was found that wandering ex-slaves were terrified of the ghost-like riders and went back to their old plantations to ask for protection and to work for a living. The Klan idea spread throughout the South as a means of scaring black vagrants into submission, and at first Klansmen employed no physical violence. General Nathan Bedford Forrest became the first national leader of the Klan when it was still a respectable, non-violent club. But the fact that Klansmen were disguised under white masks made it too easy for men to commit violent acts—whippings, burnings and even murders—in the name of the Klan.

Most Klan operations in South Carolina were in the counties where the black militia made themselves most unbearable—particularly in York, Spartanburg and Union counties. In 1870 and 1871, the black militia of Union County became so disorderly that the Klan intervened to punish them. A white man hauling a wagonload of whiskey was murdered by black militiamen because he refused to give them any of his cargo. The Klan took ten of the militiamen out and shot them. This started an epidemic in the name of the Klan, with people dressed in sheets paying off personal grudges. Finally the governor agreed to remove the militia from the disturbed counties and send competent white officials to keep the peace. From then on, there was little complaint about the Klan in South Carolina.

More respectable and effective in South Carolina were the gentlemen's rifle clubs which met for target practice on horseback. Made up largely of former Confederate officers, these clubs gave the members an excuse for meeting and carrying rifles in peacetime. Carrying banners and drilling on horseback—often with an American flag on one side of the banner to assure watchers of their patriotism—they let the lawless element know that there were crack shots able to defend honor and property when necessary. Like their Regulator ancestors, they were respectable men, on the side of law and order.

As farms and plantations started to produce once more, South Carolinians began to take heart. In 1867, phosphates (used for fertilizer) began to be mined in the state, and factories were given such good tax breaks by the carpetbaggers that new cotton and woolen mills sprang up, particularly in the Up Country. The 1870 cotton crop was the largest since the war, and year by year it grew larger. Public schools were started all over the state. (Only Charleston had done much about educating all classes before the war.) The University of South Carolina in Columbia was re-opened as a biracial normal school and turned out to be an all-black institution.

In 1872, Franklin J. Moses, Jr., the corrupt son of a good family, had been elected governor in spite of opposition of some conservative

Republicans who were beginning to be disgusted with corruption. By 1874 he had robbed the state so openly that he was made to resign. In his place the Republicans elected Daniel H. Chamberlain, a New Englander who had been attorney general and had become more conservative and honest as he saw the graft around him. In defiance of the Radicals who had elected him, Chamberlain plunged into the job of cleaning up voting fraud and enforcing economy in government. If it had not been for his insistence on racial equality, he would have been accepted by Carolinians as a good governor.

Many white Carolinians, although unwilling to join the Republican Party, were willing to cooperate with the governor to reform the Legislature. These men were known as "fusionists" or "cooperationists." Others saw the possibility of starting a whole new Straightout Democratic Party that could run against the carpetbagger Republican Party.

Northerners had finally learned of the thievery of the Radicals and their puppet President Grant. Tennessee, Georgia, North Carolina, Virginia, Alabama, Arkansas, Texas and Mississippi had all driven the Radical Republicans out of their statehouses by 1876. Two reform candidates, Samuel J. Tilden and Rutherford B. Hayes, were nominated for President of the United States. South Carolina, like Louisiana and Florida, was still under carpetbag rule but hoped to elect General Wade Hampton as governor.

Governor Chamberlain was better than most carpetbaggers, but he had brought the wrath of Carolinians down on his head when he asked President Grant for military support to "preserve order" during the election campaign, using a shooting incident at Hamburg as justification. Black militia had terrorized Hamburg and shot a white man who defied them. Five of the militiamen had then been executed by a mob of white men. It was a local racial fight, but Chamberlain was afraid it would spread. His action made many Carolinians who had stayed out of politics become determined to rid the state of Republicans.

In 1876 General Wade Hampton was nominated by the Straightout Democrats to run against Chamberlain for governor. A hero of the Confederacy, Hampton was, above all, an honest man. Strong, courageous and gentlemanly, he seemed the true embodiment of the Lost Cause. He had lost a son in action at the battle of Petersburg and had been bankrupted when his plantation was burned and his

Confederate investments devaluated. Hampton's slaves had been devoted to him, and he had shown his true concern for blacks in a published letter written in 1866, in which he advocated citizenship for blacks "on precisely the same terms as it is to be exercised by the white man. . . . Our best tactic with regard to the black man," he wrote, "is to try to convince him that we are his best friends."

Under the leadership of General Martin W. Gary (known as the "Bald Eagle of Edgefield"), the Straightouts picked Hampton as a candidate, knowing that honest, intelligent black voters would be more likely to vote for him. The Radical Republicans still held a majority of the black vote by bribery and patronage, but many former slaves were finding that the Republicans still could not be depended on in need.

In order to assure Hampton's election, however, Gary, a dyed-in-the-wool racist, knew that the Up-Country poor white vote must be courted by ungentlemanly means. The Ku Klux Klan and its white-sheeted riders were ruled out, but a fellowship of red-shirted riders could pull together the poor white vote all over the state. At Republican meetings, speakers could be shouted down by groups in red shirts. For the time being it would be the Red Shirts against the Radicals rather than blacks against whites, although race still played its part in the campaign.

A riot in Ellenton, in which two whites and forty blacks were killed, was blamed on a group of blacks trying to release a burglar from jail, but this incident was fired by tensions that were already high from election excitement. Meanwhile, Hampton campaigned with the help of both black and white Democrats. In Abbeville he was met by 3,000 mounted men, 700 of them black, and a pageant was performed. A mourning figure, wrapped in chains and representing South Carolina, threw off her chains as Hampton approached and "a young woman in pure white stood tall and stately, head uplifted and eyes shining like stars."

Hampton, by his conciliatory policy, claimed he had won over 17,000 black voters. On the other hand, black Democrats were beaten and reviled by their women and preached against in their churches. Even with strict orders to avoid violence, which would bring Federal troops, Gary's Red Shirts were able to intimidate many would-be Republicans. Hoping to avoid bloodshed, Governor Chamberlain ordered the red-shirted rifle clubs dispersed in October. In Charleston County a group of blacks, secretly armed, took advantage of the situation to shoot twenty-one unarmed white men; five were killed. To prevent retaliation, President Grant placed all Federal troops and militia at the governor's disposal.

By the time election day arrived, there had been enough blood shed and intimidation on both sides that everyone feared a massacre at the polls. The governor appointed a Democrat and two Republicans as commissioners in each county, and members of both parties were to watch polling places. There was, admittedly, fraud and intimidation by both parties, but there was no bloodshed. Hampton won by 1,134 votes, and the Democrats emerged with sixty-five house members to the Republicans' fifty-nine, while the Republicans kept eighteen senators to the Democrats' fifteen. It looked as if Reconstruction was finally over.

For a while, however, the Republicans refused to give up, and two general assemblies met—the Republicans, reinforced by Federal troops, in the State House, and the Democrats in Carolina Hall. Finally, on April 10, 1877, the Federal troops were removed by the new President, Rutherford B. Hayes, and Wade Hampton took over the governor's office.

18

The
Bourbon Era

The ten years after Reconstruction have been called "Readjustment" by some historians and the "Bourbon Era" by others.

The Bourbon Era had nothing to do with whiskey. It was named, rather, for the Bourbon kings of France who, like Wade Hampton and his associates, came to power after chaos and revolution. Critics claimed that, like the French dynasty, Carolina Bourbons had "forgotten nothing and learned nothing." Conservative, educated and respectable, South Carolina's governors from 1877 until 1886 were all former generals and statesmen of the Confederacy, members of the old ruling class. Their political appointments went to men of their own class, most of whom had gone to college in South Carolina before the war. Most Carolinians, in a state of shock and despair, clung to these former heroes because they knew and trusted them.

As soon as Wade Hampton took over the governor's office, most Northern Reconstruction officials quietly slipped away. In Washington the new South Carolina congressmen were able to make a deal: Forget the vote fraud accusations against the Red Shirts, and charges of bribery and theft would be dropped against the carpetbaggers. A huge state debt, run up during Reconstruction, was reduced by reissuing some bonds and cancelling others; this caused discontent among those (a majority of them Charlestonians) who had lost large sums. But the government was now financially sound, and its members were free from criminal guilt. The way was clear to build a new democratic state in place of the ruins left by war and corruption.

As always, the fear of black domination haunted Carolina. There were still more blacks than whites in the state, and all but a few of them were completely illiterate. They had been manipulated by carpetbaggers and then by Red Shirts, and they could be manipulated again by unscrupulous politicians. The black vote must be controlled!

Hampton and his associates were in favor of educating the illiterates, both black and white, so that they could vote responsibly. In the meantime, however, their votes must be limited. Edward McCrady, who later wrote one of the great histories of South Carolina, worked out an arrangement called "the eight box system," in which voters would place their ballots in boxes plainly marked with the names of the candidates. The boxes could be shifted around, and any votes put in the wrong boxes would be thrown out.

To educate all Carolinians, a public school tax was levied, with revenue supporting separate black and white schools. Winthrop Normal School was established in Columbia for the education of women as teachers. (Before this time, most teachers had been men.) South Carolina College, with the addition of an agricultural department and an experimental farm, became the University of South Carolina. The Citadel, which had been used as headquarters for Federal troops, was returned to the state and once more became a military college. The state penitentiary was made self-supporting by allowing convicts to be leased out to work on state and private projects. Enough money was generated by this convict labor so that the Insane Asylum was supported as well. A fence law was enacted to keep free-roaming stock from trampling farmers' crops. Another act outlawed duels as a means of settling disputes, disqualifying anyone who was involved in a duel, even as a second, from ever holding office in the state.

The Reconstruction constitution remained in effect until another could be drafted, and many of its liberal ideas were retained. But the Bourbon leaders were more in favor of taking South Carolina back to the kind of world that had existed before Secession than in creating a brave new world. Land without slaves had lost much of its value, but most of these men had contacts in the industrial and banking realms of the North. Northern money could be invested

Governor Wade Hampton III. Photograph courtesy of South Caroliniana Library, University of South Carolina.

in mills, railroads and phosphate mines to rebuild lost fortunes, create jobs and increase tax revenues for the state. The Bourbons believed in low taxes, low expenditures and little government regulation.

Poor whites all over South Carolina were able to find work in the mills, leaving worked-out farm lands and tumbledown shacks to move into new homes in mill towns. Following the lead of Gregg's project in Graniteville, mill owners promised families houses, medical care, schools, recreational facilities and very little pay. But to the poor white "lintheads," as they were called this was a bonanza. Even fifty cents a day for twelve hours work was more than they had ever had before. And since the mills hired no black workers, they did not have to worry about competition from that direction.

Black Carolinians were left to find laboring jobs on farms, on roads or railroads, or in phosphate mines, in competition with convict labor. Many blacks headed north, starting the big migration that would lead to a white majority in the next fifty years. Many who stayed became sharecroppers, and many who had obtained land under Reconstruction led bare subsistence lives on tiny farms.

To the ruling Bourbons, life was much as it had been before the war, and they encouraged sentimental stories of the Confederacy and the good old days of banjo music, moonlight and magnolias. Throughout the Bourbon period, however, there were mumblings of dissatisfaction. General Martin W. Gary was furious, after Wade Hampton's election, that he was not given an appointment as U.S. senator to pay him for his red-shirted help. General M.C. Butler, an Edgefield neighbor of Gary, was sent to the Senate instead, and the "Bald Eagle of Edgefield" became the sworn enemy of Hampton and all he stood for. When Hampton was elected to the Senate in 1878, Gary ran for governor against Hampton's choice, Johnson Hagood, and was so bitter in his campaign that many Up-Country voters turned away from him and helped to elect Hagood. This campaign was the beginning of the farmers' revolt against the Bourbons. When Gary died in 1881, he left a devoted disciple, "Pitchfork Ben" Tillman, also of Edgefield County, to organize the farmers and sweep away the Bourbon rule.

19

The Farmers' Revolt

By the early 1880s, a recession had put farmers all over the country on the edge of bankruptcy. Money was short, the price of cotton was the lowest in history, and farms were mortgaged to the hilt.

In South Carolina, the landed gentry had shown little interest in the problems of small farmers. Land was no longer the symbol of gentility. Banking, industry and railroads were being built up by those with money to invest, while the yeoman farmers, the very backbone of the land, were neglected. It was to these farmers (who, he claimed, made up three-fourths of the population) that Ben Tillman appealed.

Benjamin Ryan Tillman was one of the most colorful in a long line of South Carolina characters—"a violent man, scion of a violent, gun-toting, fairly well-to-do middle class family" from Edgefield County. A real dirt farmer with a large farm running thirty plows, Tillman knew first-hand the problems of farmers. Like most Up-Country men, he resented the rule of the Bourbons and their lack of interest in Up-Country problems. When the National Grange and South Carolina Agricultural and Mechanical Society became active in the state, Tillman became their leader.

Known as "Pitchfork Ben" because his eye had been put out by a pitchfork, Tillman told his followers that what South Carolina government needed was a good stirring up with a pitchfork. He advocated the overthrow of the Bourbon system which kept farmers under the yoke of bankers. Accusing the aristocrats of being soft on racial issues, he played on the fears and resentments of small farmers. Tillman advocated lynching, if necessary, as punishment for the rape of a white woman. Stumping through the state, speaking at barbecues in the language of his peers, he demanded a separate agricultural college, experimental stations, and farmers' institutes. Most of all, he urged voters to rid the state of "superannuated Bourbon aristocrats who are thoroughly incompetent."

Although Tillman's chief supporters were portrayed as hayseeds to gain the rural vote, a large part of their folksiness was play-acting. Almost half of his advocates were lawyers, twenty-eight percent were planters, twelve percent were professional men, and only sixteen percent were farmers.

By 1888 the Farmer's Movement had gained control of the Legislature. That same year Thomas G. Clemson, the son-in-law of John C. Calhoun, died, leaving property worth $90,000 (a huge sum in those days) to the state, on condition that South Carolina found an agricultural and mechanical college at Fort Hill, Calhoun's old plantation in the northwest corner of the state. This gift was unpopular in Columbia, where South Carolina College had become the University of South Carolina by incorporating an agricultural school and experimental farm. Conservatives realized that the state could not support two agricultural schools. The Farmers' Movement, however, took the new Ag college as a campaign issue and, in 1889, the General Assembly accepted the gift. In 1893, Clemson Agricultural College opened with 446 students, and South Carolina College (no longer the University) shrank to seventy students. Winthrop Normal School was combined with South Carolina Industrial College and moved to Rock Hill, offering women an education in teaching as well as cooking, dressmaking and other home arts.

In 1890 the Democratic candidate was still chosen in convention rather than by the primary system. Tillmanites took over the convention, "shouting down" in the old Red Shirt style anyone who opposed them. Tillman was nominated for governor, with a complete slate of "reformers." Although no one dared call himself a Republican so soon after carpetbag rule, a separate ticket was put up with Alexander Haskell, a Columbia lawyer, as an anti-Tillmanite candidate, hoping for support from black voters. Tillman won by a landslide.

The 1890 campaign also led to the founding of *The State* newspaper in Columbia, when N.G. Gonzales left Charleston's *News and*

Governor Ben Tillman, known as "Pitchfork Ben" because his eye had been put out by a pitchfork. Photograph courtesy of South Caroliniana Library, University of South Carolina.

Courier to become editor of *The State* and fight Tillmanism. The *News and Courier,* also backing the conservatives, was then edited by J.C. Hemphill, and the *Greenville News,* which had backed Tillman's agricultural ideas, now switched to the conservative side. Only the *Columbia Daily Register,* edited by Georgia journalist T. Larry Gantt and owned by the Tillmanites, supported the reformers. Gantt's earthy humor infuriated more serious editors, but it was appreciated by farmers.

One of Tillman's first acts was to see that the state legislature, which still handled the appointment of U.S. senators, replaced Senator Wade Hampton, the almost sainted aristocrat, with John L.M. Irby of Laurens County, who was "not known for his saintliness." Other political plums and patronage jobs went to Up-Country friends and supporters, especially those from Edgefield.

In 1892 Tillman used the same tactics to win the governorship again, arousing class consciousness among farmers by disparaging both aristocrats and mill hands, and arousing the fear of black dominance and race mongrelization.

During his second term, Tillman seemed to have broadened his horizons. His administration passed the state's first law regulating work hours for mill workers, although he claimed no interest in the "damned factory class." Mill owners cried that reducing shifts to ten hours a day, sixty-six hours a week, would ruin them.

But the program which led the state to near revolt was the State Dispensary. In 1892 a bill prohibiting all whiskey sales in South Carolina was introduced in the legislature. Governor Tillman, seeing a chance for increased revenue and knowing how hard it would be to enforce prohibition, added an amendment setting up a state liquor board that would sell liquor in controlled stores. Almost as soon as the bill was passed, there was furious opposition by both strict prohibitionists and those who wanted no control. To prevent the selling of bootleg whiskey, a constabulary was set up to enforce the law.

In 1894, a riot known as the Whiskey Rebellion broke out in Darlington when some constables sent to search for illegal whiskey became involved in a private argument between two Darlington citizens. One of the constables was shot and killed, and the crowd of Darlington citizens who had gathered to protest the search pitched into the fight. One man was killed and several wounded on both sides before the constables were driven out of town. Tillman then declared the counties of Darlington and Florence in a state of insurrection; when he ordered out the state militia, many troops refused to obey. The governor's own guards, in Columbia, were then assembled and told they must go to Darlington, but they stepped out of their ranks and stacked their arms at the governor's feet. The Zouaves (an elite militia company) were told by Bishop Capers that it was not their duty, and they refused to obey the governor's call. Citizens organized and confronted troops to persuade them to refuse to go. Tillman ordered all troops who refused, to be dishonorably discharged.

Finally, some troops were assembled and put on the train for Darlington. They arrived to find that the liquor dispensaries in Darlington and Florence had been broken into by mobs and the liquor stolen and wasted, but that everything was now quiet and under the control of the Darlington Guards. After all the excitement in Columbia, Pitchfork Ben's militia had not been needed.

Like many of Tillman's policies, the State Dispensary stirred up more controversy than it deserved. But Pitchfork Ben was a controversial figure who seemed to arouse passionate approval or antagonism in people. Some of his programs did start badly-needed social reforms, and he did make the small farmer conscious of his political clout. In many cases, however, it was a matter of using bad means to a good end. Class and racial prejudices were stirred into hatred by emotional harangues for political ends. Tillman is important in history not so much for what he accomplished as for his method of accomplishing it. His successful strategy has been copied by Southern politicians for the last 100 years to keep the status quo intact and fill the pockets of enterprising demagogues.

One such demagogue, probably the caricature of all demagogues, was Coleman L. Blease of Newberry, an early follower of Tillman who branched out on his own and was denounced by Pitchfork Ben. The son of "one of the best families," Coley Blease went to Newberry College and then received a law degree from Georgetown University. Seeing a chance to control the mill vote, he later assumed an ungrammatical way of speaking, using vulgarity, obscenity and rowdy humor to make himself popular with mill workers.

Although he never had a real program to help the "little man," Blease had the hypnotic appeal of a carnival barker, shouting against blacks, aristocrats, newspapers, or anyone else he could set up as a scapegoat. In the governor's office he dressed in swallow-tailed coat and striped trousers, burlesquing the aristocrats to the joy of his poor white followers. They loved him and twice elected him governor (and later U.S. Senator); yet he opposed laws for the limitation of working hours and compulsory education (which would have stopped child labor), and vetoed legislation that would have instituted factory inspections for safety and health conditions. Ignorance and prejudice kept his followers faithful, and they failed to realize that he was working against their best interests. The only benefit that Blease brought to the poor whites was a sense of importance which stemmed from their ability to use their votes to influence elections. With this power, they were one up on the blacks.

The black vote had been practically eliminated by now. In 1895

Tillman had pushed through a new state constitution that avoided colliding directly with the Fifteenth Amendment but effectively kept blacks from the polling booths. Wade Hampton, who was still a spokesman for the conservatives although no longer a political power, spoke out against the voting clause. Blacks "ask only the rights guaranteed them by the Constitution of the United States," Hampton said. In a state with 782,321 blacks and only 557,807 whites, however, the memory of Reconstruction was still vivid, and there was only one possible outcome.

The 1895 Constitution was carefully constructed so that it restricted illiterate black voters while allowing illiterate whites to slip through. Every registered voter was required to be literate, but those who could not read or write were given three years to get lifetime registration certificates by proving to the Registration Board that they could "understand" the Constitution when it was read to them. White registrars had the power to pass illiterate whites and fail educated blacks who did not measure up to unspecified standards of "understanding."

Anyone disenfranchised for illiteracy could vote if he could show ownership of $300 worth of property. On the other hand, anyone guilty of certain crimes—such as receiving stolen goods, wife-beating and bigamy (crimes for which more blacks than whites were convicted)—could be disenfranchised. Such serious crimes as murder were not included on this list. A man had to be twenty-one and a resident of the state for two years, the county for one year, and the precinct for four months (blacks tended to move about more than whites). In order to register, he also had to have paid a poll tax six months before elections. As N.G. Gonzales said in *The State*, "Ignorance is only dangerous to Tillman when it is black ignorance."

The Constitution of 1895 was one of Tillman's last shows of political strength in state affairs. By the time Pitchfork Ben went on to the U.S. Senate, his choice for governor, John Gary Evans, another Edgefield man, had been elected. In 1896, when Evans ran for U.S. Senator, he was defeated by a progressive-minded conservative, Judge Joseph H. Earle. When Earle died, he was succeeded by John L. McLaurin of Marlboro County, who had once been a Tillmanite but now favored "more factories and material progress and less political strife." McLaurin's disagreements with Tillman led to a fistfight on the floor of the U.S. Senate and Pitchfork Ben's censure by that body in 1902. When Theodore Roosevelt heard of the fight, he withdrew a White House dinner invitation, which made Tillman his enemy for life.

But as the years rolled by and South Carolinians returned him to the Senate over and over again, Pitchfork Ben mellowed until, by the time of his death in 1918, he was a highly-esteemed senior statesman, chairman of the Naval Affairs Committee and a supporter of the war effort.

20

The Growth of
Industry and Power

As politics swung the power from conservatives to rabble-rousers and back again, the people of South Carolina went on from day to day, thankful for the end of Reconstruction and trying to rebuild their lives and homes.

Victorian times, including the Gay Nineties, are always painted as comfortable, easy-going days of carriages and gabled houses with wide, vine-covered porches, of elaborate dinners and Gibson Girl clothes. This picture was true for the fortunate upper classes in South Carolina, but it leaves out the darker side—the poverty, ill health and near-starvation of poor Carolinians.

When the big plantations were broken up after Emancipation, their owners invested in banking, railroads and factories. Farmers solved the labor problem by taking on tenants who would work for a percentage of the crop. Since cotton was the best-selling cash crop, most farmers tried to grow cotton on land that was already worn out. In the southwestern states, land was still fertile, and bumper cotton crops were being produced. The price of cotton was so low that neither landlords nor tenants made a real living from farms.

When cotton mills were built, mainly in the Piedmont, labor was drawn from the poor whites who had lived on marginal small farms of their own or as tenants or sharecroppers. Used to living in shacks far from their neighbors, most of the millhands were glad to move into new mill housing. Small and bare though the houses might be, each had a yard where vegetables could be grown. With mill owners providing schools, recreation facilities, health care, a company store and church, the mill workers' lives seemed full of everything desirable. If they had to work twelve hours a day for low wages, they had worked from dawn to dusk on the farms for no wage at all. The mill owners allowed their children to work and were glad for the few extra pennies a day, even though the children had no time left for school. After all, the children had worked on the farm. The whole family also enjoyed the social life of the mill village, which they had never had before.

But the longer they worked in a mill, the dimmer their memories of back-breaking labor on the farm became. At least their work had been outdoors in the "old days," with trees and creeks and growing plants, and a man could drop his hoe and go fishing without a supervisor ordering him around. With the heat and lint and high prices at the store, wages began to seem lower and lower. When rabble-rousers like Blease promised help, the mill people were ready to vote for whatever these new leaders wanted. Unfortunately, their votes did little to lighten their load.

The farmers—and they still made up a majority of the white population of the state—were individuals, descendents of liberty-loving pioneers. By 1890 the average farm had shrunk to ninety acres, and sixty-one percent of the farmers were tenants. But they had kept their liberty, even though many farmers lived on the poverty level. With country schools few and far between, most had never learned to do more than read and write, and many farmers still had to make their mark when voting. They enjoyed such simple pleasures as church socials and picnics, quilting bees (a holdover from frontier days), and summer camp meetings that drew people from miles around. Country people were hard workers, but with cotton prices down to five cents a pound, they had to mortgage their farms; now their independence and their very lives were threatened. The Grange and the South Carolina Agricultural and Mechanical Society gave them hope, and Ben Tillman—with his promise of farm reform and education in modern methods of agriculture—gave them a hero to follow.

During the period between Reconstruction and World War I, several events helped to improve the farmers' lot. Tillman's opening of Clemson Agricultural College in 1893 marked the beginning of an era of better farming methods. Better seeds were developed in

Hartsville by James L. Coker and his son David, so that stronger plants could be grown. Other crops were added to cotton as cash earners. Charleston's *News and Courier* publicized tobacco and even distributed free seeds, while *The State* advocated the growing of corn. Federal legislation just before World War I helped vocational and agricultural education by sponsoring county home and farm demonstrations. By the end of the war boom, many farmers were able to pay off their mortgages and live in comparative comfort.

In 1900 Charleston was still the largest city in South Carolina, with a population of about 56,000. Columbia had a population of about 21,000; Greenville and Spartanburg had nearly 12,000 each; and all the other cities in the state had less than 6,000. The largest towns were usually the county seats, on whose tree-bordered streets lived lawyers, cotton buyers, doctors, dentists and clergymen as well as general storekeepers, livery stablemen and saloon keepers—before Tillman's Dispensary made liquor sales illegal except by the state.

Charleston, as always, had the most cosmopolitan and sophisticated society. This port city had launched a public school system in 1856, paid for by a city tax. Christopher G. Memminger, a German

Horse and buggies congregate in front of the Coca Cola Bottling Company in Columbia, 1911. Photograph courtesy of South Caroliniana Library, University of South Carolina.

orphan raised by a wealthy Charleston family and one of the most influential state legislators before Secession, established a system by which the whole body of white youth, male and female, would be educated at free common schools in subjects which should fit them for producing things and making money. By 1860, after the establishment of a Normal School and a City High School, Charleston city schools had an enrollment of 2,786. Although interrupted by the war, the Charleston schools were far ahead of any others in South Carolina for many years. The Citadel and the College of Charleston attracted well-to-do young men after the war, when finances and distrust of Yankees kept them from going north for an education. In 1886 an earthquake struck Charleston, killing ninety-two people and doing over five million dollars worth of damage. Relief funds totaling $792,733 were sent to help the victims; almost $300,000 came from New York and Massachusetts, the two states which had been most active in Reconstruction in the area. The "decorations" on many of Charleston's old houses today, up near the eaves, are the ends of long rods stuck through the walls to strengthen masonry weakened by the earthquake.

Although war, fire, earthquake and frequent hurricanes failed to discourage Charlestonians, the dread of fever—thought to come from the bad air in the swamps around the city—drove some to the beaches, where the wind blew away the miasma, and many more to Up-Country sulphur springs and the North Carolina mountains each summer. Some wealthy Charlestonians who had summered in Newport, Rhode Island before the war renewed old friendships there. Even after the last major outbreak of "stranger's" fever in 1876, Low-Country people habitually headed for the hills until after the first frost. When Walter Reed discovered that the disease was carried by mosquitoes which bred in stagnant water, the annual summer exodus was justified. Drainage and sanitation finally conquered the disease completely, but even today Charlestonians may be found in the mountains each summer, living in cottages built by their ancestors.

In winter and early spring, Charleston streets were busy with carriages full of well-dressed city-dwellers having a good time. Any excuse for a ball, a tea or a concert drew the cream of society. Lavish meals of seafood and game in many courses were served by black waiters in livery. When land was no longer the basis of respectability, money from Northern banks helped to bolster the fortunes of the gentry.

Charlestonians made headlines during the 1890s for refusing to obey Tillman's liquor law and selling liquor openly when and where they pleased. After Pitchfork Ben put the city under martial law, Charleston's mayor appointed metropolitan police commissioners who promised to enforce the Dispensary law and sent Tillman's men back to Columbia. There were no more flagrant violations of the liquor law, but Charlestonians continued to imbibe as always.

Up-Country men resented the city's defiance of the law and its sense of superiority. After all, with Columbia the state capital and growing like wildfire, Charleston could no longer claim to be the only city in the state. What's more, Charleston's growth rate was not equal to that of the other cities.

Located in the center of the state, Columbia was growing in spite of having been barbarously ravaged by Sherman and occupied for years by a carpetbag legislature. Columbians had begun rebuilding almost before Sherman's troops were out of sight; they had quietly ignored the Yankee legislators and soldiers, rebuilding their homes and churches and caring for their friends and neighbors who had lost everything. All during the war, Low-Country refugees had flocked to Columbia, fearing attacks from the sea. Many of these families remained in the capital and helped to rebuild.

When South Carolina College and the South Carolina Agricultural and Mechanical Institute had been forced to enroll blacks during Reconstruction, South Carolina College's white faculty and students had all resigned. A Northern faculty was then recruited by the Legislature, and the college became predominantly black. At the end of Reconstruction, the College was quietly closed, and its faculty sent back up North, leaving only the black Agricultural and Mechanical College supported by the state. When South Carolina College re-opened, its faculty members were white, many having been there before Reconstruction. Only white students were enrolled.

Cotton mills and rebuilt railroads had given Columbia a boost. As capital of the state, the city had all the excitement of legislative controversies, and its hotels and boarding houses were filled when the General Assembly met. The State, established in Columbia in 1891, was one of the most influential newspapers in the South. The State Insane Asylum, one of the first three in the United States, had been established in 1828 in a fortress-like fireproof building designed by Robert Mills and was a model of enlightened treatment for its time. The penitentiary, rebuilt after the fire, provided prison labor for roads and sanitation work around the city. Columbians could be justly proud of their ability to rebound.

Greenville, Spartanburg and other Up-Country towns grew rapidly with the establishment of industry, mainly cotton mills. At first powered by water, the mills were soon converted to coal and steam. To carry coal, railroads had to be built, and short lines soon led into small towns all over the state; many of these lines were financed by Northern capital. The Charleston and Hamburg Railroad had been one of the first in the country but had, like most other lines, been destroyed by Sherman's troops. Until the automobile came into use in the early 1900s, small towns depended almost entirely on railroads for growth.

But more significant than the railroads or the automobile to South Carolina's growth was the development of hydroelectric power. As usual, it was the dreams of forward-looking men that made the miracle possible.

James Buchanan Duke, born on a tobacco farm in North Carolina, had made hundreds of millions of dollars by the time he was fifty-eight years old. Living in New York and known already as the tobacco tycoon of the world, he was looking for another outlet for his endless energy when he had to call in a doctor to treat his sore foot. Dr. Walker Gill Wylie, the very successful New York surgeon who treated his foot, was originally from Chester, South Carolina. As the two Carolinians swapped yarns, Dr. Wylie mentioned the hydroelectric power plant that William Lee, from Lancaster, South Carolina, had built for him as an experiment on his plantation near Chester. Buck Duke was also experimenting with the use of water-power to generate electricity on his estate in New Jersey.

As early as 1894, a hydroelectric plant had been established on the Rocky River near Anderson; another had been built at Postman Shoals on the Seneca, where Dr. Wylie's dam builder, William Lee, had worked as resident engineer. At Duke's request, Lee was called to New York. With enormous enthusiasm, he painted a picture of the limitless opportunities offered by the Catawba-Wateree river system, where a series of dams could be built to produce electric power to run mills and light homes. Lee's vision fascinated Duke,

President William Taft speaks briefly to the crowd gathered at the railroad station in Orangeburg in 1912. Photograph courtesy of the Orangeburg County Historical Society.

who loved large-scale projects with plenty of challenges. Lee returned to South Carolina with $100,000 from the doctor and the tobacco man to buy land for the first dam, as well as a promise of millions to develop the Catawba-Wateree in a series of dams from the mountains to the fall line. The Southern Power Company (later the Duke Power Company), the result of the dreams of three dynamic men, became the first major hydroelectric superpower system in the world.

Until the TVA system was built with Federal funds in the 1930s, the Catawba-Wateree remained the greatest power river in the United States, electrifying Carolina homes and factories while other states still depended on gas and kerosene for light and power. Lakes formed by the dams became fishing and boating paradises for tourists. Later, when the Saluda and Savannah followed the lead of the Catawba, the whole geography of the state was changed. Now mills and other industries could flourish in every little village without depending on a nearby river or railroad, and tourists could leave the Northern cold and enjoy Southern lakes.

This abundance of power helped South Carolina plunge into the war effort in 1917.

21

The Conservative Progressives

In the years before World War I, Carolina politics had swung between Bourbon and Populist administrations. During the four years of Cole Blease's governorship, he had so angered the responsible voters of South Carolina that, by 1914, they were ready for intelligent, constructive government. Blease had recklessly pardoned criminals, made vicious personal attacks on public officials, opposed all school attendance laws and labor legislation, defended lynching to the point where he said, "To hell with the Constitution!" at a Southern governor's conference, and criticized President Woodrow Wilson, who was very popular in South Carolina. Even Senator Ben Tillman was against Blease's candidacy for governor and quietly backed Richard I. Manning, a lawyer, planter, businessman and cultivated gentleman. Blease's populist followers, mostly farm tenants and textile workers, were the only ones who continued to support him for the U.S. Senate and his candidate, James G. Richards, for governor.

Conservative Bourbons considered Manning a safe choice, but he was also supported by the middle-class Progressives and the leading newspapers. After Manning won the election, the Bourbons were surprised to find that he planned to push forward progressive reforms. During his years as governor, he accomplished more in social and economic reform than anyone in South Carolina history. The textile mills were required to pay wages on a weekly basis, limited to sixty hours a week, restricted from hiring children under fourteen, and required to submit to arbitration in labor disputes. Farmers were provided with improved markets and better agricultural education. A state Board of Charities and Corrections was formed to oversee the state hospital and the penitentiary, and a highway commission was established to supervise and promote the building of roads.

With Woodrow Wilson (the first Southerner to be elected since Reconstruction) in the White House, South Carolina could join the rest of the Progressive South in a tide of social reform. The fact that Wilson had lived in Columbia as a youth, when his father was a professor at the Presbyterian Seminary, made him almost a Carolinian, and his conservative-progressive ideas made him popular in the state.

With the outbreak of war in Europe, many Carolinians of German descent, and some of Irish Catholic descent, were sympathetic to the Kaiser and opposed Wilson's aid to England and France; but by the time Congress voted to enter the war on the side of the Allies, even German and Irish Carolinians rallied to the flag. Cole Blease guessed wrong about Carolinians' ideals and denounced Congress for declaring war, accusing Governor Manning of stealing "the souls and bodies of your boys." But South Carolinians black and white went enthusiastically to work to win the war.

South Carolina soldiers were, as always, distinguished in their patriotism. A total of 64,739 served in the armed forces, and 2,085 died. Governor Manning's six sons were all in the service, and one was killed in action just before Armistice. Six out of the seventy-eight Congressional Medals of Honor went to South Carolina men. South Carolina blacks served overseas in work battalions and in the First American Army that fought near Verdun, proving that black men could fight for their country as well as work in laboring jobs.

At home, army installations were built in South Carolina and other Southern states to take advantage of the climate. Camp Jackson at Columbia, Camp Sevier at Greenville, Camp Wadsworth at Spartanburg, Parris Island's Marine Recruiting Depot, and Charleston's Marine Corps Supply Depot brought from forty to sixty thousand men in uniform to the state. Surprisingly, little strife resulted, and local merchants prospered.

The war boom had raised the price of cotton and textiles and caused a runaway expansion in the lumber industry. For a while, at

Governor Richard I. Manning, who accomplished during his years as governor more in social and economic reform than anyone in South Carolina history. Photograph courtesy of South Caroliniana Library, University of South Carolina.

least, the state was wealthy enough to pay its debts and push forward the Progressive goals: good roads, good schools, good health and good government (good government meaning as little as possible). Labor relations and race relations were better left alone.

But these two touchy subjects were very hard to ignore. It was hard to keep the veterans down on the farm after they'd seen Paree—or even Camp Jackson or the warplants. Army pay, or pay in the munitions factories, was more than most tenant farmers had seen in a lifetime. Army life, although segregated, was much freer and less race-conscious than life at home. And when troops went overseas, there was no racial discrimination at all.

Though he worked conscientiously for the improvement of health, education and financial progress, Woodrow Wilson did not believe in social integration of blacks and whites. Southern blacks who had believed Wilson would help them towards equality had already given up hope and begun to move north where wages were higher and segregation less rigid.

Steel companies and other Northern industries encouraged the black migration, transporting trainloads of workers to camps in the North where they could stay until they could be distributed to work areas. At first South Carolinians were happy to see them go, to cut down the number of destitute and migrant unemployed. But it was usually the good workers who left. Within twenty years so many blacks had left South Carolina that whites were a majority. When shortages of labor began to hamper Carolina industry, *The State* asked its readers, "If you thought you might be lynched by mistake, would you remain in South Carolina?" An Up-Country paper warned that if the South wanted to keep its great black labor supply, it must change its treatment of blacks.

In 1919 a convention of black South Carolinians met and planned a drive to register every eligible black to vote, hoping to become a balance of power between white factions. A long list of grievances was aired, including Jim Crow laws and inequality of schools and salaries.

Rumors of impending race riots terrified whites everywhere, and the Ku Klux Klan was revived in Atlanta and spread all over the United States. These white-sheeted riders had no connection with the Reconstruction days organization except for their costumes and the name. They not only frightened blacks but also persecuted Jews and Catholics; finally they began beating people who didn't go to church or strayed from their marriage vows, deteriorating as their Regulator forebears had 200 years before. When the Klan resorted to torture and murder as well as savage beatings, it began to be shunned by its members. Still, politicians were afraid to proceed against it—at first for fear of lost votes, and later for fear of physical injury. But by 1925 the Klan had become so disreputable that it lost most of its members and faded from sight, except for a short revival to oppose Al Smith, the Catholic presidential candidate, in 1928.

More worrisome to conservatives that black activism or the resulting Klan revival was the stirring of labor unrest. Low wages and docile millhands had influenced many Northern mills to move south, and the New South ideal of industrialization depended on keeping the poor white labor supply in hand. "Labor of purest Anglo-Saxon stock," a Spartanburg advertisement read, "Strikes unknown."

Paternalism, the obligation of every mill owner to take care of his people, had always given the workers a sense of belonging to the company family. Mill owners, like Antebellum planters in the early days, took a personal interest in the problems of their workers. But social workers and ministers began to call attention to long hours, low wages, employment of women and children, and lack of labor representation. National labor unions tried to take advantage, and the United Textile Workers sent organizers south. In 1919 the union called for a general strike in the textile mills to push for a forty-eight-hour week. Carolina workers who struck were fired, or the mills closed. But with the postwar slump of the early twenties, workers were afraid of losing their jobs and the movement collapsed. Most Up-Country workers, true to their independent Scotch-Irish blood, wanted nothing to do with national unions. Disputes could be settled with their bosses without bringing in "communists and bolsheviks."

In the mid-1920s, mill owners, anxious over low textile sales, made the mistake of bringing in outside "efficiency experts" to increase profits. Workers were furious at what they called the "stretch-out" suggested by these busybodies. Fifteen South Carolina mills struck against the stretch-out, but not under union guidance. A Greenville striker told a newsman, "We don't want no organizers from outside. We're doin' this ourselves." South Carolina mill operators received delegations and eliminated or modified stretch-outs. The owners and workers were satisfied, and the strike ended.

South Carolina's state government conducted an investigation of workers' grievances—and was the only state in the United States to do so. A committee from the legislature, including a former textile worker, Olin D. Johnston, found that the mills were "putting more work on the employees than they can do." Both state and industry worked for reform.

With the stock market crash and the beginning of the Depression in 1929, South Carolina was one of the first states to feel the crunch as people stopped buying textiles. But although times were hard and unemployment high, the farmers and textile workers, used to living on low wages, seemed to be able to scratch out a living where people in wealthier states were unable to cope. And when Franklin D. Roosevelt brought his New Deal philosophy to the presidency, his programs brought financial relief that seemed like wealth to black and white workers who had "never had it so good."

Roosevelt was very interested in the South, perhaps because of his stay in Warm Springs, Georgia, where he had been treated for polio, but most likely because of the number of Southerners in his government. James F. Byrnes of South Carolina was one of his most trusted advisors.

Byrnes, unlike most Carolina politicians of his day, was not a member of an old Carolina family. Born in Charleston after his father's death, he had been reared by his widowed Irish Catholic mother, a talented dressmaker. Much in demand among stylish Charleston ladies, she was able to send Jimmy and his sister to parochial school, though Jimmy studied shorthand instead of going to high school, so that he could help support the family. As secretary-stenographer in a Charleston law firm, he was encouraged by one of its partners, Benjamin Rutledge, to study history, economics, politics and law.

James Byrnes moved in 1900 to Spartanburg and later to Aiken, where he and a friend bought the *Aiken Journal and Review.* His editorials championed white supremacy but were against lynching and the disruption of Southern society by rabble-rousers. Elected a circuit solicitor of the seven-county district along the Savannah— "the damndest, gamecockingest, liquor-drinkingest, nigger-shootingest, sinfullest place in South Carolina"—he worked for fair trials for all, black and white alike. His desire for social order and fairness, and his engaging personality, gave him a victory in the Congressional election of 1920 and, in 1930, a seat in the U.S. Senate. Throughout his years in Congress and the Senate, as Roosevelt's personal advisor, as Governor of South Carolina and as Justice of the U.S. Supreme Court, Byrnes was known as a liberal but not a radical. He advocated truly equal facilities for black students, although he was against integration. He fought the Ku Klux Klan and worked for equal Depression relief for Southern workers, but he discouraged irresponsible welfare spending.

As the New Deal became more entrenched, Southerners began to worry about rising Federal control of property, labor and credit. State and local governments seemed to have less and less responsibility. When Roosevelt proposed the creation of fifty new Federal judges and six new justices to water down conservative power in the Supreme Court, the Southerners in Congress revolted. They felt that the proposal threatened the Constitution, states' rights and white supremacy. Although the plan was never put into effect, it had started a split in the Democratic Party that has never really healed. Even James Byrnes began to oppose Roosevelt's spending programs. Southern Democrats began to join conservative Republicans in opposing ultra-liberal legislation and in trying to put some of the responsibility for relief on local communities.

In 1938 Roosevelt decided to gain control of Congress by eliminating conservatives, both Republican and Democrat. Campaigning throughout the country for liberal candidates, he antagonized voters by opposing well-loved statesmen who had supported him in his early days. In the South, in most cases, Roosevelt's candidates lost. In South Carolina, Roosevelt's candidate, Governor Olin D. Johnston, "the mill boy governor," was running for the Senate against Ellison D. Smith, who had been in the Senate since 1908. "Cotton Ed" Smith was a politician of the old rabble-rousing school who had won his first campaign for the Senate riding around the state on a farm wagon loaded with cotton, dressed in a farm hat, and denouncing Wall Street and the Cotton Exchange. His loyalty, however, had always been with planters and industrialists, and his votes had always been conservative. Opposing Roosevelt's "purge," James Byrnes called on Federal officeholders to back Smith. Voters of all opinions turned out, determined that South Carolinians would not be pressured by a Yankee, even Franklin D. Roosevelt. The night that Cotton Ed won, he led a red shirt parade to the Wade Hampton statue on the State House grounds, proclaiming, "No man dares to come into South Carolina and try to dictate to the sons of those men who held high the hands of Lee and Hampton."

By this time, however, South Carolina and the world had a more dangerous dictator to contend with. As Adolph Hitler's war machine rolled across Europe, it became more and more clear that the United States would again try to save the world for democracy. War plants and military establishments sprang up once more throughout the South, and Depression and welfare programs could be forgotten. Labor shortages, rather than unemployment, became the problem of the day. Roosevelt, as commander in chief, could depend on the support of all patriotic Americans. South Carolinians once more rallied to their country's call and served with conspicuous bravery.

22

Industrialization
and Integration

By the end of World War II, the South had been so changed, both economically and socially, that there could never be a return to old customs and ideals. During the war, income grew 250 percent, new industries were established, and workers, both black and white, learned new skills. Money poured into Southern banks, and people of all classes became used to a high standard of living.

South Carolina, like the rest of the South, had to adjust to the change. Industry, encouraged by the climate and labor supply, but also by the tax breaks given by Carolina communities, remained and multiplied after the war. As foreign industry was able to rebuild under the Marshall Plan, foreign-owned manufacturing plants were built, particularly in the Piedmont. So many foreign languages are now heard on the streets of Spartanburg that a native suggested signs be put up, "English spoken here," in shops.

Labor organizers, while not as successful as in the North, brought unions to many industries. South Carolina, however, has kept an open shop law. Farm tenancy, as it was known after Reconstruction, has almost disappeared, with many farms now owned by large insurance companies and other absentee landlords who provide machinery and fertilizer for competent managers to make farming pay. The cotton fields have decreased, giving way to soybeans and cattle pastures. Millworkers are now guaranteed at least a Federal minimum wage and live in homes of their choice, often on small farms.

The biggest change, however, has been the integration of the black population into all phases of South Carolina life.

During World War II, the Committee on Fair Employment Practices (FEPC) had acted to assure the training of blacks in skilled jobs to help remedy the shortage of trained labor in war plants. Employers, anxious to keep these skilled people, relaxed their attitudes toward segregated restrooms, eating facilities and housing. When the war was over, black workers were not about to go back to Jim Crow days, and Federal laws began to be passed, assuring them of equal treatment. Meanwhile, although army units were still segregated, the Navy had begun integrating. When the Air Force split off as a separate branch, it was integrated. Within a few years, the Army was integrated, too.

South Carolinians were slow to yield to the national trend. When the Supreme Court struck down the legality of the Democratic white primary in 1947, the South Carolina Legislature enacted laws that cut all state ties to the primary, making it a private club where only white members could vote. By the end of the 1960s, however, many Democrats were so dismayed by the liberal acts of the national Democratic Party that they voted Republican. J. Strom Thurmond—an Edgefield man like so many other political figures— had long been an enemy of liberals. In 1948, when Harry S. Truman was running for President on a Civil Rights platform, Thurmond was nominated by the Dixiecrat Party and ran against him. During his governorship and his years in the Senate, Thurmond had been true to the white supremacy, states' rights ideal. In 1964 he switched to the Republican Party and has served in the Senate as a Republican ever since.

When the Supreme Court outlawed compulsory segregation in public schools, the state legislature approved a bill authorizing the closing of all schools to prevent integration and repealing the compulsory school attendance law. By 1962 there was still no integration, but by the early 1970s integration had begun. There were clashes in many communities, but the program was successfully carried out. The hatred and fear that erupted in many states was rare in South Carolina. Mills now hire black as well as white operators, and all Federal regulations are obeyed. Buses and restaurants, restrooms and swimming pools are open to all races.

Without forsaking pride in their history, South Carolinians have become part of the new world of progress. Once dependent upon textiles and agriculture for most of their revenue, they have diversified their industry to include highly technical electronics as well as more traditional products. Taking advantage of their warm climate and rich heritage, they have made tourism a major financial asset. Urban renewal has gone hand in hand with historic preservation, and recreational planning with water resource development. As South Carolina prepares to enter the twenty-first century, she is very much a part of the American Dream.

23

Achievers in the
Arts and Sciences

Much has been said about wars and political strife, pioneers and planters, Indians and slaves. *The South Carolina Story* has hit the high spots of action and adventure, but the artists and artisans, the scientists and writers have been neglected in order to get on with the tale. Many of these individuals were involved in the action, but they should be remembered also for making life a little better and more beautiful with their work.

From the very beginning, the quality of Carolina life was shaped by the craftsmen who settled between the Ashley and the Cooper. Builders of houses and churches copied the London architecture of Sir Christopher Wren but turned the houses sidewise to catch the evening breeze and added porches overhanging walled gardens. Few names survive, but it is known that Samuel Cardy and a "craftsman named Gibson" built St. Michael's Church, while John and Peter Horlbeck built the Exchange. William Johnson, Tunis Tebout and other blacksmiths fabricated the lacy ironwork for the porches as well as shoeing horses and repairing wagons. Artists such as George Flagg and Benjamin Hawes worked as house painters to make a living, painting portraits and teaching art classes in their spare time. Jeremiah Theus painted crests and coats of arms on coaches to get a start in Charles Town.

Theus came to Carolina from Switzerland with his father and two brothers, to help found Orangeburg. By 1740 he had moved to Charles Town and placed an advertisement in the *South Carolina*

Gazette which is typical of those placed by artists and artisans of the period: "Notice is hereby given, that Jeremiah Theus Limner is remov'd into the Market Square near Mr. John Laurans Sadler where all Gentlemen and Ladies have their Pictures drawn, likewise Landskips [sic] of all sizes, crests and Coats of Arms for Coaches or Chaises. Likewise for the Conveniency of those who live in the Country, he is willing to wait on them at their respective plantations."

Thomas Elfe, a leading cabinetmaker before the Revolution, is representative of the careful craftsmen who left thousands of beautifully-made pieces to be handed down to posterity. Although most furniture was copied from the styles of English cabinetmakers, Elfe developed a style of his own that has made Charleston pieces unique. He was famous for the graceful frets on his furniture, using such secondary woods as cypress, cedar and poplar, as well as the fashionable mahogany.

By the 1770s many artisans of Charles Town had become wealthy, had invested in land and fine homes, and were anxious to be equal, in other ways, to the "merchant-planter class." By custom, craftsmen could not sit in the Assembly, and in 1702 the Fellowship Society was organized, allegedly to "afford relief to many poor distressed persons in this province." But although it did help the poor and its own members and paid for the education of deserving young scholars, the Society was important also as a gathering of artisans dissatisfied with aristocratic rule. It was this group that became the core of the Liberty Boys who met with Christopher Gadsden under the big oak tree in Izaac Mazyck's pasture.

These meetings were faithfully reported by the *South Carolina Gazette,* the newspaper created by Louis Timothy (or Timothee), a French Huguenot, in 1732 and carried on after his death by his wife Elizabeth until his son Peter could take over the publication and the printing business. When Peter Timothy died, his wife Ann, who had worked with him, took over and published the *Gazette* all through the Revolutionary War and until it was replaced, in 1800, by the *Courier.* Copies of this early paper, now preserved on microfilm, are a goldmine to writers and historians.

A less formal source of information, but one which gives a more colorful picture of life, are the diaries and letterbooks of Carolinians. (Letterbooks were collections of letters received and copies of letters sent in answer.) Many of these diarists and correspondents were

Mrs. Thomas Lynch, painted by Jeremiah Theus, 1755. Photograph courtesy of Reynolda House, Museum of American Art, Winston-Salem, N.C.

women who, with servants to care for house and family, had time to use their talents to put their observations on paper. Judith Manigault's letters to her brother give readers a lucid picture of the life of very early settlers. Eliza Lucas Pinckney's letterbooks, journal and cookbook have been saved, and her ideas and opinions, as well as her observations of nature and theories of agriculture, are as fresh today as they were 250 years ago. She has been quoted by historians, beginning with David Ramsay in 1808, and even today her informal style and sense of humor make her work delightful for its own sake.

A friend of Eliza Pinckney, Dr. Alexander Garden, was one of Carolina's earliest scientists. His letters to European scientists were illustrated by drawings of Carolina plants and flowers, and he shipped hundreds of specimens from the swamps and fields to be studied in England. Scientific societies in Europe asked him to become a member, and the gardenia, a cultivated version of the cape jessamine, was named for him.

Another writer who was more famous for his actions than for his writings was Charles Woodmason. His *Journal* and *Sermon Book* give rare descriptions of the backcountry before the Revolutionary War. Woodmason's letters to the Charles Town *Gazette*, many published under pen names, were finally responsible for bringing schools and courts to the backwoods.

After the Revolution, Dr. David Ramsay wrote his *History of South Carolina,* compiled from first-hand accounts of people who were there. This is still a valuable reference work for historians.

Carolinians have always been history-conscious and have written reams to prove it. A few such writers stand out as authors rather than as recorders of dates and events. One of these is Harriot Horry Rutledge Ravanel, Eliza Pinckney's great-granddaughter, who wrote, among others things, a biography of Eliza and a history of Charleston which is so cozy and conversational that it makes the reader feel a part of Charleston society and familiar with the people who made history there.

William Gilmore Simms was also a historian but is better known for his novels about South Carolina in the days between the Revolutionary War and the Civil War. The novel by Simms that is most frequently read today is *The Yemassee*, about early colonial days. His *History of South Carolina* for school children, revised by his granddaughter, Mary Simms Oliphant, has been in use in South Carolina schools for many years.

Another author of this period between wars, Charles Fraser, is better remembered for his miniature paintings of members of prominent Charleston families. The character shown in the delicate lines of his paintings provides insight into the impact that his subjects had on history.

Out of the Civil War came numerous first-hand stories of battles and biographies of generals, but some of the most interesting accounts are found in the diaries of women of the time. Mary Boykin Chesnut, the wife of a Confederate general, seems to have been in the very place where things were happening all through the war. Her dry humor and sense of the ridiculous make her writing appeal to modern readers. Published as *A Diary From Dixie*, her reminiscences have been reprinted in the last few years.

Emma LeConte, who was also in Columbia throughout Sherman's disastrous visit, describes in her diary the burning of the city as seen from the South Carolina College campus. Her account gives the reader a sense of the emotional stress, anger, despair and then the determination to survive and rebuild that motivated the people of Columbia.

Emma LeConte's father, Joseph LeConte, taught at South Carolina College before the war and served the Confederacy as a chemist. He was well-known nationally for his work in various sciences and wrote books and articles on geology, binocular vision, physiology and evolution. Although LeConte left South Carolina during Reconstruction, when the college was taken over by carpetbaggers, and became a professor at the new University of California, Carolina is proud of his work and considers him her own.

Floride Clemson Lee, granddaughter of John C. Calhoun and daughter of Thomas Clemson, kept a diary of her life in Washington, D.C. when her father was Secretary of Agriculture. The diary continues through the Civil War and the trials of Reconstruction after her return to South Carolina. Her descriptions are supplemented by drawings of her friends and of the fashions of the day.

Floride's father, during his term as head of the U.S. Agriculture Department, had been responsible for the importation of new strains of seeds and plants from Europe. Clemson College was one of the first institutions to encourage scientific agricultural practice. In this same tradition, James L. Coker and his son David worked on the scientific hybridization of seed. Their strong hybrids helped South Carolina farmers compete in the world market.

History, biography, fiction, poetry and drama have flowed from the pens of South Carolinians over the years, and it would be impossible to mention more than a few. During the 1920s and 1930s, there was a real renaissance of writing, after the hard years of Reconstruction when there was no "leisured" class to write or paint. The Poetry Society of South Carolina, under the leadership of

DuBose Heyward, through its *Yearbook,* encouraged poets and novelists, including Beatrice Ravanel, Josephine Pinckney, Drayton Mayrant, Herbert Ravanel Sass, Hervey Allen and John Bennett, whose books were published nationally. Heyward himself wrote many tales of Low-Country life, often focusing on the Gullah-speaking blacks of the Carolina coast. His novel *Porgy,* about Charleston's black community, was the basis for *Porgy and Bess,* one of the most enduring works of the American musical stage.

Like Heyward, Julia Peterkin chose to write about South Carolina's black community. Writing from Lang Syne Plantation, she focused on the lives and ways of the plantation's Gullah inhabitants in such works as *Green Thursday* and *Black April.* In 1928 Julia Peterkin was awarded a Pulitzer Prize for her novel *Scarlet Sister Mary.*

Another outstanding writer of prose and poetry was Archibald Rutledge, who became the state's Poet Laureate in 1934. Although he spent thirty-three years as head of the English department at Mercersburg Academy in Pennsylvania, Rutledge's writing transfigured his memories of Carolina with a nostalgic glow that made readers appreciate the beauties of home. He is best remembered today for his beautiful descriptions of life in the woods, fields and plantations of his native state, in such works as *Home by the River.*

One artist who comes to mind in this period is Elizabeth O'Neill Verner, whose paintings in oil and pastel and superb etchings of life in Charleston portray the atmosphere of the Low Country and its inhabitants with love. The author of several books in addition to her graphic art, Verner was the mother of Elizabeth Verner Hamilton, herself a talented poet.

Carolina has always produced talented artists. Now, with black Carolinians having an equal opportunity for self-expression, there should be a broader scope of artistic creativity in the state. It is important for Carolinians to know about their heritage and incorporate the good things of the past in their work today. Only by knowing the past can we explain the present and anticipate the future.

Bibliography

Bass, Robert D. *The Gamecock.* Sandlapper.

——— , *The Green Dragoon.* Sandlapper.

——— , *Ninety-Six.* Sandlapper, 1978.

——— , *The Swamp Fox.* Sandlapper, 1976.

Blassingame, John W. *The Slave Community.* Oxford Press, 1972.

Bodie, Idella, *South Carolina Women,* Sandlapper, 1978.

——— , *The Story of Archibald Rutledge.* Sandlapper, 1980.

Bowers, Claude G. *The Tragic Era.* Houghton Mifflin, 1929.

Brown, Richard Maxwell. *The South Carolina Regulators.* Belknap of Harvard U. Press, 1963.

Cashin, Edward J. and Heard Robertson. *Augusta and the American Revolution.* Richmond County Historical Soc., 1975.

Cenam, C.W. *The First American.* Harcourt Brace, 1971.

Chandler, David Leon. *The Natural Superiority of Southern Politicians.* Doubleday, 1977.

Clark, Thomas D. and Albert D. Kerinan. *The South Since Appomattox.* Oxford U. Press, 1967.

Commager, Henry Steele. *The Blue and the Gray.* Bobbs-Merrill, 1950.

Cooke, Donald E. *Fathers of America's Freedom.* Hammond, 1969.

Davis, Burke. *Sherman's March.* Random House, 1980.

Dumond, Dwight Lowell. *Anti-Slavery.* U. of Michigan Press, 1961.

Dunn, Richard S. *Sugar and Slaves.* UNC Press, 1972.

Ezell, John Samuel. *The South Since 1865.* Macmillan, 1963.

Farley, M. Foster. *An Account of Stranger's Fever in Charleston, 1699–1876.* University Press of America, 1978.

——— , *Newberry County in the American Revolution.* Newberry Historical Committee, 1975.

Gerson, Noel B. *The Swamp Fox.* Doubleday, 1967.

Graff, Henry F. and John A. Krout, *The Adventure of the American People.* Rand McNally, 1968.

Greg, Rt. Rev. Alexander. *History of the Old Cheraws.* The Reprint Co., 1965.

Guess, William Francis. *South Carolina.* Harper, 1960.

Hall, Walter and Robert Albion. *A History of England and the British Empire.* Ginn and Co., 1953.

Hilborn, Nat and Sam Hilborn. *Battleground of Freedom.* Sandlapper, 1970.

Hilton, Capt. William. *Voyage to the Carolina Coast.* Reprint, Hilton Head Pub. Co., 1976.

Hirsch, Arthur Henry. *The Huguenots of South Carolina.* Duke Univ. Press, 1928.

Hollis, David W. "Cole Blease: The Years Between Governorship and the Senate," *S.C. Historical Magazine,* Jan. 1979.

Hooker, Richard J. *The Carolina Backcountry on the Eve of the Revolution.* UNC Press, 1953.

Hudson, Charles. *The Southeastern Indians.* U. of Tennessee Press, 1976.

Johnson, Capt. Charles. *History of the Robberies and Murders of the Most Notorious Pirates.* Geo. Rutledge & Sons, Ltd., 1926.

Jones, Katherine M. *Heroines of Dixie.* Mockingbird Press, 1975.

— — —, *Port Royal Under Six Flags.* Bobbs-Merrill, 1960.

Jones, Lewis P. *South Carolina: A Synoptic History for Laymen.* Sandlapper, 1975.

— — —, *The South Carolina Civil War of 1775.* Sandlapper, 1975.

Jones, Virgil Carrington. *The Civil War at Sea.* Rinehart-Winston. 1962.

Lamson, Peggy. *The Glorious Failure.* W.W. Norton, 1973.

Lumpkin, Henry, *From Savannah to Yorktown.* USC Press, 1981.

Marion, John Francis. *The Charleston Story.* Stackpole Books, 1978.

Marriott, Alice. *The First Comers.* Longman, Green, 1960.

Marsh, Kenneth F. and Blanche Marsh. *Plantation Heritage.* Biltmore, 1962.

Middleton, Margaret Simons. *Jeremiah Theus, Colonial Artist of Charles Town.* USC Press, 1953.

Moore, Winfred B., Jr. "James F. Byrnes: The Road to Politics, 1882–1910," *S.C. Historical Magazine,* April 1983.

Oaks, James. *The Ruling Race.* Knopf, 1982.

Oliphant, Mary Simms. *The History of South Carolina.* State, 1917.

Olmsted, Frederick Law. *The Cotton Kingdom.* Knopf, 1970.

Osborne, Anne. "Pirates Off the Carolina Coast," *Augusta Chronicle,* July 18, 1971.

Owens, Leslie Howard. *This Species of Property.* Oxford U., 1976.

Petit, J. Percival. *South Carolina and the Sea.* S.C. Ports Authority Centennial Project, 1976.

Pinckney, Elise, Ed. *The Letterbook of Eliza Lucas Pinckney, 1739–1762.* UNC Press, 1972.

Pringle, Elizabeth W. Allston. *Chronicles of Chicora Wood.* Christopher, 1940.

Rogers, George C., Jr. *Charleston in the Age of the Pinckneys.* U. of Oklahoma, 1969.

Rose, Willie Lee. *Rehearsal for Reconstruction.* Vintage (Random House), 1964.

Savage, Henry, Jr. *River of the Carolinas: The Santee.* UNC Press, 1968.

Smith, Alice R. Huger and D.E. Huger. *Charles Fraser.* Garnier, 1967.

Smith, T. Marshall. *Legends of the War of Independence.* Brennan, 1855.

Smith, Warren B. *White Servitude in Colonial South Carolina.* USC Press, 1961.

Snowden, Yates. *History of South Carolina.* Lewis, 1920.

Stern, Philip Van Doren. *An End of Valor.* Houghton Mifflin, 1958.

Thompson, Henry T. *Ousting the Carpetbagger from South Carolina.* Negro Universities Press, 1969.

Tindall, George B. The Emergence of the New South, 1913–1945. LSU Press, 1967.

——— , *South Carolina Negroes, 1877–1900.* USC Press, 1970.

——— , *Trinity Church, Columbia, S.C.* The State Co., 1937.

Van Doren, Mark, Ed. *Travels of William Bartram.* Dover, 1955.

Wallace, David Duncan. *South Carolina: A Short History, 1520–1948.* UNC Press, 1951.

Wheeler, Richard. *Voices of the Civil War.* Crowell, 1976.

Wilkins, Robert P., Ed. *South Carolina History Illustrated,* 4 vols. Sandlapper, 1970.

Willimon, William H. *Lord of the Congaree.* Sandlapper, 1972.

Workman, W.D., Jr. "Know Your State," *The State* newspaper, 1980–82 (a series of articles).

Wright, Louis B. *South Carolina: A Bicentennial History.* Norton, 1976.

Historical Novels and Other Fiction About South Carolina

The following books will, I hope, help make history come alive for many readers. I was not fond of the subject during my school days, and it was only after I began reading historical novels that I fell in love with the heroes, heroines and events of the past.

Many of the books on this list are out of print, but readers should be able to find them at public libraries.

Colonial Period

Few, Mary Dodgen. *Azalie of Bordeaux.* Greenwood Books, 1973. A tale of backcountry life in colonial times.

Leland, John A. *Othneil Jones.* Lippincott, 1956. About a young Cherokee fighting with Marion in Tennessee.

Osborne, Anne. *Wind From the Main.* Sandlapper, 1972. The story of Anne Bonny, pirate.

Pinckney, Josephine. *Hilton Head.* Farrar-Rinehart, 1941. Dr. Henry Woodward's adventures, including Charleston's founding.

Sass, Herbert Ravanel. *Emperor Brims.* Doubleday, 1941. About an Indian uprising before the Revolution.

Simms, William Gilmore. *The Yemassee.* USC Press, 1974. Indian troubles in early colonial days.

Tracy, Don. *Carolina Corsair.* Dial, 1955. The adventures of Blackbeard the pirate.

Revolutionary War

Bristow, Gwen, *Celia Garth.* Crowell, 1959. Story of an orphaned seamstress in Revolutionary Charleston.

Chapman, Maristan. *Rogue's March.* Lippincott, 1949. A military adventure during the Revolutionary War.

Davis, Burke. *The Ragged Ones.* Rinehart, 1951. Campaigns of Morgan and Greene against Cornwallis.

Lancaster, Bruce. *The Phantom Fortress.* Little, 1950. Adventures of the Swamp Fox's men.

Miller, Helen Topping. *Slow Dies the Thunder.* Bobbs, 1955. Battles of Charleston and King's Mountain.

Roberts, Kenneth. *Oliver Wiswell.* Doubleday, 1940. Campaigns of the Revolution, including the siege of Ninety-Six.

Sabatini, Rafael. *The Carolinian.* Houghton, 1925. Sea adventures during the Revolution.

Antebellum Carolina

Coker, Elizabeth Boatwright. *Daughter of Strangers.* The life of an octaroon girl on a Carolina plantation.

Heyward, DuBose. *Peter Ashley.* Farrar, 1932. A Southerner's struggle with his conscience before the Civil War.

Sass, Herbert Ravanel. *Look Back to Glory.* Bobbs, 1933. Life in coastal Carolina before the Civil War.

Simons, Katherine, *The Red Doe.* Appleton, 1953.

Stern, Philip. *Drums of Morning.* Doubleday, 1942. Political events and emotional concerns that led up to the Civil War.

Tracy, Don. *Cherokee.* Dial, 1957. An Indian's life under white rule.

Civil War Period

Brick, John. *Jubilee.* Doubleday, 1956. About Sherman's march.

Coker, Elizabeth Boatwright. *La Belle.* Dutton, 1959. The life of Marie Boozer, Southern belle turned Yankee camp follower.

Feuille, Frank. *The Cotton Road.* Morrow, 1954. About running cotton through the blockade.

Griswold, Frances. *A Sea Island Lady.* Beaufort, 1939. Yankee occupation of the sea islands.

Haas, Ben. *The Foragers.* Simon & Schuster, 1962. The search for supplies by a family and Confederate troops.

Jacobs, Thornwell. *Red Lantern on St. Michael's.* Dutton, 1940. Life in Charleston during bombardment.

Mason, Van Wyck. *Our Valiant Few.* Little, 1956. Blockade of Charleston and Savannah.

Mason, Van Wyck. *Proud New Flags.* Lippincott, 1951. Adventures with the Confederate Navy.

Roark, Garland. *Outlawed Banner.* Doubleday, 1956. Adventures of blockade runners.

Slaughter, Frank. *Lorena.* Doubleday, 1969. The story of a woman managing a plantation during the war.

Tracy, Don. *On the Midnight Tide.* Dial, 1957. More adventures of blockade runners.

Yerby, Frank. *Captain Rebel.* Dial, 1965. The story of a blockade runner.

Postbellum to Modern Times

Fox, William Price. *Moonshine Light, Monshine Bright.* Lippincott, 1967. The story of a boy and his father's still in Columbia, S.C.

Fox, William Price. *Southern Fried.* Lippincott, 1968. Humorous stories about Carolina characters in the recent past.

Heyward, DuBose. *Mamba's Daughters.* Crowell, 1929. The story of a black woman's life.

Heyward, DuBose. *Porgy.* H. Doran, 1925. Novel about black Charlestonians from which *Porgy and Bess* was derived.

Peterkin, Julia. *Black April.* Bobbs-Merrill, 1927. Stories of Gullah blacks on a country plantation.

Peterkin, Julia. *Scarlet Sister Mary.* Bobbs-Merrill, 1928. Pulitzer Prize-winning novel of Gullah life.

Pinckney, Josephine. *Three O'Clock Dinner.* Viking, 1945. South Carolina family life.

Robertson, Ben. *Red Hills and Cotton.* Knopf, 1942. Country life during the Depression.

Verner, Elizabeth O'Neill. *Stonewall Ladies.* Tradd Street Press, 1963. About elderly ladies in Charleston.

Index